SUNSHINE PATRIOTS

SUNSHINE PATRIOTS

PUNISHMENT AND THE VIETNAM OFFENDER

By
G. DAVID CURRY

UNIVERSITY OF NOTRE DAME PRESS
NOTRE DAME   LONDON

Library of Congress Cataloging in Publication Data

Curry, G. David.
  Sunshine patriots.

  Bibliography: p.
  Includes index.
  1. Vietnamese Conflict, 1961–1975 — Draft resisters —
United States. 2. Vietnamese Conflict, 1961–1975 —
Desertions — United States. 3. Military service,
Compulsory — United States. 4. Punishment — United States.
I. Title.
DS559.8.D7C87 1984   959.704′33′73   81-40450
ISBN 0-268-01706-9

Manufactured in the United States of America

Contents

Foreword

The term *Vietnam offender* is a euphemism, but one which permits a social researcher a very broad and comprehensive approach to violations of law and administrative procedures by those who sought to avoid military service during that conflict. Research on the Vietnam offender is an essential contribution to the historical and socio-political record. The available statistical and quantitative materials present a complex and entangled body of information which is difficult to understand fully.

David Curry's study is an important contribution to the writing on the Vietnam conflict. He is a careful and self-critical scholar who has sought to put into sharp perspective the types and magnitudes of offenses involved against the Selective Service System. He has also described the scope of the government's enforcement effort. He has thoroughly and carefully worked over the official and documentary statistics. Of special importance is his reanalysis of the sample surveys conducted by the Center for Civil Rights of the University of Notre Dame.

But David Curry's efforts are hardly limited to ordering and clarifying the available statistical data. From his perspective of a struggle for objectivity, he has sought to present an interpretation of the sequence of events involved; that is, the sequence of events at the individual level and the sequence of events for American society as a whole. Curry disposes of simpleminded explanations and instead examines the effective realities.

The importance of the analysis is not that he has laid to rest forever the neat and pat explanations. Such explanations will still be believed by those who will avoid close examination of his analysis. His contribution rests on the fact that he demonstrates that the individual person — not all but a large percentage — had the ability, if interested, to control whether and how he served in the armed forces. There was a national Selective Service System with an elaborate administrative and law enforcement backup; but there was also an informal system which made it possible for the individual to bargain and to manipulate the rules and procedures. We are truly dealing with an American response to a bureaucratic organization. And it was not simply the privileged who worked their way out or devised approaches of avoidance; such initiatives were spread in varying degrees throughout the social hierarchy.

Initial research conducted on the Vietnam offender was strongly motivated by policy goals and by the desire to influence the actions of President James Carter. Much of the research made use of the broadest terms of reference in order to achieve the maximum relief by means of presidential action. This was especially true for the studies conducted by the Center for Civil Rights of the University of Notre Dame, which, therefore, is to be commended for encouraging David Curry to take a second look at their data, reports, and analyses. This study is the result of such a second examination.

In the end, 10,000 persons received relief by President Carter's action. This result disappointed deeply the pro-amnesty advocates, while of course offending the anti-amnesty advocates. The issue of the Vietnam offender cut deeply into the grain of U. S. society, and the aftermath still persists in a subdued fashion. I believe that David Curry's analysis helps to clarify the problem of linkages between social research and public policy, both in general and specifically in the case of the Vietnam offender.

One must recognize that policy recommendations rest heavily on political and moral values. Research cannot necessarily resolve such issues, although it can contribute to their clarification. I had the privilege of observing and discussing with the University of Notre Dame study group, and with Father Theodore M. Hesburgh, who was their prime mover. The assumptions under which the University of Notre Dame study was conducted were two-fold, and these assumptions decisively influenced their policy strategy and the recommendations they pressed on President Carter, recommendations which to a considerable extent were disregarded. The staff made two assumptions, both of which were designed to increase the number of persons who would obtain relief by presidential action. First, the war in Vietnam was implicitly immoral; therefore to resist it was a moral act. Second, the Selective Service System treated the youth of the United States unfairly, unequally, and almost by chance. In the absence of equal treatment, the offender had a powerful case to have charges and convictions against him dismissed.

These arguments were in my view irrelevant to the issue of amnesty. The first argument only served to inflame passions and made pro-amnesty steps more difficult. The second argument was narrowly legalistic and hardly well understood, as well as of dubious relevance. In fact, it led military personnel and individuals who supported the war in Vietnam to believe that the claim was being made that the military were in error in dealing with the Vietnam offender. Again, such reasoning served to inflame passions and was irrelevant to the central issue of amnesty.

The issue of amnesty rests not on the findings of social research, but on compassion and religious and moral considerations. The case for amnesty by the president, and I speak of the president and not of the courts, rests on compassion for those who had been punished and those who had already suffered. It is true that some had suffered very little; but others had already suffered more than enough. They had in effect been punished by dishonorable discharge and by other ways. In short, the argument for clemency was compassion for those who had been punished and who needed to have an end to their punishment. Dishonorable discharge was a form of punishment with a type of indeterminate sentence.

After a number of years of normal civilian life, the dishonorable discharge could and should be eliminated. Interestingly enough many military personnel were prepared to accept this argument. The idea of indeterminate and unending sentence was repugnant.

Instead of compassion, political and legalistic arguments were put forward. But such arguments did not permit the president to launch an extensive amnesty. The consequences of the recommendations of the University of Notre Dame study group were contrary to their intended goal. The result was to limit the scope for pro-amnesty steps.

David Curry's study therefore helps to point up the real linkage between social research and social public policy. Sound research helps to clarify the issues which have to be faced. However, social research is no substitute for effective and acceptable moral principles. Because he keeps this basic point in mind, David Curry has made a lasting contribution to understanding the costs and aftermath of the Vietnam conflict.

Near South Side   MORRIS JANOWITZ
University of Chicago
Chicago, Illinois
October 1983

Preface

Morris Janowitz was the first scholar whom I heard refer to the Vietnam conflict as the Second Indochina War. Such a designation places the politico-military venture in nation-building within its world historical context by recognizing that it was no more than the second unsuccessful attempt by a Western power to maintain a system of allied regimes in the resource-rich peninsula of Southeast Asia. But the world historical truth is not necessarily an identical truth for the people of the United States of America who, second only to the people of Southeast Asia, felt the political, social, and economic realities of the war with sometimes devastating impact. *Sunshine Patriots* deals with only one aspect of the war, military service and its avoidance, but within that one phenomenon can be found encapsulated all those social forces which brought turbulance and change into a decade of American life.

The writing of *Sunshine Patriots* shattered stereotypes for me. I, as most Americans, pictured the draft avoider and the deserter in terms of the media-generated images at my disposal. Draft avoiders were resisters who sewed American flags on the seat of tattered jeans and made articulate philosophical statements to their draft boards just before they slipped into the new "underground railway" to Canada or Sweden. Deserters were wiley cowards who, when their craftiness failed them, abandoned their comrades in the face of the enemy or even the possibility of facing the enemy. They too, in my imagination, lived the good life in the bountiful northern forests of other lands. While holding true in a few cases, these images could not have been greater distortions of the statistical profiles generated by my research.

Perhaps the greatest surprise to me was the discovery that overly represented among deserters were Vietnam veterans who had satisfactorily completed their tours in the combat zone and had returned to the States. At the time of greatest personnel commitment to the war, only fifteen percent of active duty troops were assigned to Vietnam. In the sample of deserters examined herein, twenty-seven percent went to Vietnam and at least twenty-four percent successfully finished their tours.

The image of the sly, crafty deserter does not retain its currency in this research — not when approximately one-third of the sample of deserters studied are revealed to have been inducted under Project 100,000 — a special program for integrating the mentally deprived into the mainstream of American society. While a large portion of the low IQ soldiers inducted by Project 100,000 went to Vietnam, the statistics herein show them to constitute the largest group of non-Vietnam related desertions. Images of men taking several months to meet the mental requirements of the Army's two-month basic training and thereafter unable to master the simplest of tasks cannot possibly fulfill our desire for Vietnam-era villains.

Poverty and race were major factors in the social change which characterized the Vietnam period, and poverty and race are found to be major factors in military service and its avoidance. Bureaucratic structures which reflected the world-views of their New Deal creators ground into the sixties generation with disconcerting effects on both the generation and the bureaucracies. The two chief bureaucratic actors in this scenario were the Selective Service System and the Department of Defense personnel system, and both receive considerable attention in the analysis that follows.

As a new generation of bureaucrats begin to build new institutions to take the place of the old, they might do well to keep in mind the new profiles of deserters and draft avoiders which are emerging as sociologists reanalyze the Vietnam experience.

A large group of deserters are men who served in Vietnam. True, as many analysts point out, there was little place "to run to" in Vietnam, but why run at all upon return to stateside? An acceptable explanation is as follows. The meaningless regulated routine-for-its-own-sake which dominates life on stateside military bases may have constituted a source of irritation with which it was impossible to cope for many veterans who had just returned from the "unreal" life-and-death world of Vietnam service. For 365 days he had counted down for a "freedom" that did not resemble spit-shined shoes and duty rosters on the one hand and a mixed if not hostile reaction from the public on the other. Going absent-without-leave was a socially harmless act in comparison to more violent reactions to the situation. Tentative research is showing that many Vietnam veterans had difficulty readjusting to civilian jobs, colleges, and families. Why should they have coped any better with stateside miltitary routine? *see chart*

Only seven percent of the desertions in this study deserted upon receipt of orders for Vietnam. The remainder of the deserter population is composed of a wide range of social misfits. "Losers" in military society bear a not-so-remarkable resemblance to "losers" in civilian society. The spawn of troubled families, poverty, and oppressed minorities fill the ranks of Vietnam-era deserters just as they filled the ranks of World War II deserters.

The "popular" World War II desertion rates were just as high as those for Vietnam with one exception. The desertion rate for Marines in World War II was comparatively low with a high in 1944 of 6.9 per one thousand personnel. In 1968 the desertion rate for Marines was the highest of any branch of service, 30.7 per one thousand personnel.

Analyses of the workings of the Selective Service System and the military personnel system reveal many legal ways to avoid military service and Vietnam service. The competence necessary to "beat the system" is however shown to be associated with social class background.

The statistical analyses reported herein were conducted in 1977 when many techniques such as the causal modeling of qualitative dependent variables, discriminant analysis, and canonical correlation were unavailable or unknown to the author. While this research extends the work of Baskir and Strauss from the univariate to the bivariate level, many more questions will be answered by multivariate analyses of these data sets.

Acknowledgments

Several institutions and a number of people deserve special credit for this research. The Ford Foundation provided financial support. Father Theodore M. Hesburgh, whom I have never met, is responsible for this project's existence. Administratively the Center for Civil Rights at the University of Notre Dame and the Inter-University Seminar on Armed Forces and Society at the University of Chicago were of invaluable aid. Larry Baskir and Bill Strauss conscientiously provided the initial course which I have followed, and I hope their excellent books on this subject will be widely read. Don Kommers provided spiritual and intellectual encouragement as valuable as his administrative skills. Norma Silvers, Ellen Stern, and Elaine Perry performed an important and similar role at the three different universities where this work took place. Sue Zwick and Bill Wise linked me to the tremendous foundation of work on this subject which has already been done at the Center for Civil Rights. Warren Beatty, Scott Sibley, and Katherine MacDonald greatly facilitated my access to the Computation Center at the University of South Alabama. Morris Janowitz, my teacher and friend, brought me to the task, guided me to its completion, and nursemaided me through its more difficult moments. Carol Darden, Lori Harris, Caroline Jumper, William Paul, and Leverne Westry provided me with research assistance and an ever patient audience to my developing ideas. Rita Kopcinski, librarian at the Center for Civil Rights, repeatedly proved of invaluable assistance during my work. Sue Nall, Nancy Hanks, Fran Johnson, and Janette Curry all provided some of the typing. Two editors have poured an inordinate amount of energy into the publication of *Sunshine Patriots*. John Scanlan of the Center for Civil Rights conducted a painstaking preliminary editing, and even shared his home with me one cold, work-filled Christmas vacation in South Bend. Still, publication of this book would not have been a reality without the commitment of Richard Allen, who in addition to his considerable editing, demonstrated amazing patience and emotional determination in carrying out the completion of this project. At the time I conducted my research and prepared my first draft, Janette Curry was my wife. She deserves special mention for her continuing unique contributions and support. All of the above have my love, respect, and gratitude. They must, however, be exempted from criticisms of this work's shortcomings. Those are by rights my own.

Sunshine Patriots was scheduled for release in March 1982. All that remained were a few simple revisions. During the spring and summer of 1981, the Vietnam veterans in my life encouraged me, against my better judgement and career goals, to serve one more 365 day tour for the Vietnam generation by acting as team leader of the Gulf Coast Vietnam-Era Veterans Outreach Center in Mobile, Alabama. In fall 1981, all my projects including the final revisions on *Sunshine Patriots* were postponed while I threw myself into the struggle of Alabama Vietnam-Era veterans to provide ourselves with decent services and a much-deserved place of respect in contemporary society. On February 17, 1982, twenty minutes after I had made a speech thanking the crowd for at last welcoming us "home" with the grand opening of the new center, I, along with other vet center employees and activists, was informed that both Alabama Vietnam Vet Centers were being seized by federal and state authorities pending the conclusion of a massive undercover operation into the Vietnam veterans movement in Alabama.

Now after several grand jury investigations, criminal indictments, and three months "observation" in the Federal Correctional Institution at Tallahassee, Florida, I owe my physical freedom to make last minute revisions to the University of Chicago and James Coleman who have provided me with gainful employment and academic resources while I wait out my appeals.

I wish to dedicate *Sunshine Patriots* to my father, Minter Glen Curry, and my late mother, Martha Kemp Curry.

1

Theoretical Perspectives

This book is a study of desertion during the Second Indochina War. It will dig into some of the evidence which remains unsorted from those years of social upheaval and political crisis. The work of Lawrence Baskir and William Strauss on the same subject provides the foundation for this effort. Two data sets which they used will be subjected to further statistical analysis, with an emphasis placed on the relationships between pairs of social characteristics for large groups of men.[1]

Such research is by nature sociological. Sociology, as are the other social sciences, is restricted to specific procedures for the presentation of information. A "pure" recitation of information is not necessarily "good" sociology. If a set of social facts are to be of relevance, there should be some connection between these social facts and the body of knowledge which already exists about the subject under study.

Here, the general subjects are military institutions and the relationships of individual humans to those institutions. A more specific concern is the manner in which citizens attempt to avoid military service, and more particularly how such avoidance was manifested during America's involvement in Southeast Asia. To place this effort within the context of relevant social science research requires a brief historical review of previous work and the establishment of theoretical parameters to be used in interpreting the findings which are to follow.

The single largest collection of social research on human beings as instruments of war is to be found in the two volumes of *The American Soldier* by Samuel Stouffer and four other social psychologists. In attempting to sum up their experience in terms of its indications for the future needs of social research, they list the following points:

1. Social science requires theories, at least of some limited generality, which can be operationally formulated such that verification is pos-

sible, and from which predictions can be made successfully to new specific instances.

2. Such theories demand that the objects of study be isolated and accurately described, preferably by measurement.

3. Once the variables are identified, the test of the adequacy of the theory, in comparison with alternative theories, must be rigorous, preferably evidenced by controlled experiment, and preferably replicated.[2]

An attempt to follow these suggestions will be the format of later chapters in this book. The purpose of this chapter will be to frame the present research within three more general theoretical approaches to the phenomena under study.

The first is a *functional* theory in which the military is considered to be a social system with certain operational needs. Principal among these needs is the integration of the individual into the military unit. If the individual does not fit into this scheme, he is defective and must be processed and labeled as such. This theoretical perspective has emerged from and been sustained by a rich tradition of empirical research.

The second theoretical theme is a derivative of *conflict* theory which is best represented by the works of Karl Marx and the diversified tradition which has been inspired by him. Though its process is essentially dialectical, its viability as an approach to describing draft avoidance and desertion behavior must rest on the results of statistical analyses.

Finally a *rational* model of behavior is utilized in an effort to describe the degree to which an individual's purposive actions affected his chances of performing military service or of being assigned to Vietnam. The complete reductionism often associated with a behavioristic model is avoided by placing rational action within its social context and by examining the degree to which social background and organizational constraints limit human behavior.

None of these theoretical themes is exclusive of the others. In fact, they are complementary to the extent that the first is institutional in orientation, the second concerns the dialectical interplay of individual and institution, and the third takes the perspective of the individual who is attempting to cope with a fixed institutional setting. None of these theoretical perspectives is being offered as "value free." As a matter of fact, part of the point of offering three separate theoretical perspectives is to allow the reader to contrast the distinct value assumptions associated with each.

A Functional Theory of Institutional Needs

That enduring social formations have "needs" is an idea which received its first sophisticated presentation in the work of Emile Durkheim.[3] Just as a living organism has working parts whose processes of operation make sense only in the total context of the organism, so it is that the separate aspects of a social system may make sense only within the context of the survival of the total social system. That these social functions can sometimes be met through "societal" action or rational planning is an insight usually credited to Max Weber. The most advanced form of societal action is the bureaucracy with its written rules and records which often transcend the participation of any of the human actors who compose it.[4] Military institutions constitute one of the oldest kinds of bureaucracies. It should not be surprising, then, to find rationally-designed procedures for meeting the survival needs and goals of military institutions.

For some time, the military as an institution has struggled to use scientific research to meet its organizational needs. One recognized institutional need of a military organization is the process by which an individual who is a product of a nonmilitary social order can be integrated into the structure of a military unit. Since individuals in modern societies are seldom brought up to be soldiers, the social integration of new recruits is a persistent military problem. Among social scientific works on the American serviceman in World War II, three bear special significance for the problem of social integration.

The first is S. L. A. Marshall's *Men Against Fire*. Though Marshall's theme is an essentially technical one focusing on the organizational mechanics of infantry units engaged in combat, his basic conclusions about the nature of why men fight proved vital to the effectiveness of organizational adaptations which emerged from his analysis. Marshall demonstrated that for a citizen soldiery in battle the crucial factors are not individual but social. In the formula for success in battle, he argued, could be found a smaller degree of innate individual aggressive will and courage and a greater portion of collective solidarity and interpersonal cohesion.[5]

The vital ingredient in effective military organization was for Marshall the creation of social unity. While Marshall described the structure of command procedures necessary for the fostering of such unity, his findings imply that the essential complement to efficient command is a type of soldier who can most easily adjust to membership in a collectivity.

Marshall's basic assumptions about the factors underlying effective military organization allow a more useful interpretation of the findings of Stouffer and his co-researchers in *The American Soldier.* Throughout the course of World War II, this group of social psychologists conducted surveys on the morale, military career success, and reactions to combat of the men who composed the air and ground forces. Using four indicators of positive adjustment to military life, the authors demonstrated the positive correlation of these attitudinal items with military performance and then set out to show the background characteristics associated with each criterion. In looking at a cross section of service personnel, Stouffer and his colleagues found some significant variations in certain dimensions of adjustment when marital status, age, and education were taken into consideration. Still, among the general population, none of these social background characteristics was associated with any universal pattern of maladjustment. In other words, they found that while married men demonstrated a significantly lower personal commitment to service in comparison to unmarried men, they showed about the same level of satisfaction with military status and job. On the other hand, better-educated men were more likely to show a significantly higher degree of personal commitment and a significantly lower level of military status and job satisfaction than their less well-educated comrades. Stouffer and his colleagues' conclusion was that a number of differing sociological profiles were associated with successful integration into a military unit.[6]

When, however, Stouffer and his colleagues applied their methodology to comparing the general population of armed services personnel to a group of men who had committed absence offenses, they found that the absence offenders were younger, significantly less well-educated, and more likely to be married than the general population of personnel.[7] In interpreting these findings, it is possible to regard these background variables as reflecting underlying social pressures which determine the likelihood that an individual can adjust to military service. Education can imply both a higher socioeconomic background and an ability to adapt to institutionalized processes of socialization. Age can be assumed to be an indicator of maturity and general stability, while marriage (at the time of World War II) can be regarded as membership in a primary group which could serve to "distract" the serviceman from his duties as a soldier. From the work of Stouffer, et al, tendency toward disintegration in armed forces units during World War II can be attributed to the relationship between the individual serviceman and the collectivities in which he was enmeshed.

In classical social theory, primary groups are those held together by affective ties, while secondary groups are those in which membership is governed by more instrumental motivations. The relative importance of these two types of associations in military organization was the central issue of Edward Shils and Morris Janowitz's "Cohesion and Disintegration in the Wehrmacht in World War II."[8] In attempting to discover what psychological strategies would prove most effective against enemy military personnel, these two researchers discovered that the solidarity of primary group formations in military units was the crucial factor in the durability of those units in combat. The resistance of Nazi prisoners to allied propaganda was shown to be directly related to the strength of their affective ties to their fellow soldiers. Again, a vital factor in World War II desertion was demonstrated to be the degree to which the individual could be integrated into the collectivity.

The theoretical conclusions of Shils and Janowitz were tested by researchers in both the Korean and Vietnam conflicts. For Korea, Roger Little found the one-to-one relationship of two "buddies" to be the most important social unit among men in combat situations. Rotation policies which limited both the period of time that a man spent in Korea and on the front lines severely restricted the degree to which larger communities of men could develop. Still, certain types of men whom Little labeled "heroes" and "duds" were less likely to be integrated into such buddy relationships.[9]

Rotation was also a factor in Vietnam. Earlier in the war, when men were being sent to Vietnam as members of already formed units, Charles Moskos found a pattern of primary and secondary group ties comparable to that described by Shils and Janowitz,[10] but as the war dragged on, rotation became an individual phenomenon and morale dissolved, producing a previously unrecorded type of primary group. In his analysis of in-depth interviews with ninety Vietnam veterans, John Helmer notes that when Stouffer and his colleagues asked World War II G.I.'s how they got through the roughest moments, the universal answer was prayer. Helmer feels that support of a nonspiritual sort was available to the American soldier in Vietnam as was evidenced by a high incidence of alcoholism and other forms of drug abuse. Primary groups in the latter years of Vietnam, he argues, were formed on the basis of drug preference. The use of alcohol, marijuana, and to some extent the opiates was social. In the case of the latter, the secrecy and supply problems associated with its use may have been responsible for the forging of the primary group solidarity which led to the widespread troop revolts of 1971 as well as to the strength which kept the American forces from totally disintegrating in the final years of the conflict. Not only substance abuse, but all forms of deviance, play a functional role in military institutions, argues Clifton Bryant in his socio-historical study of crime in a military context. In a war that many civilian observers regarded as internationally "criminal," Bryant's examination of disciplinary infractions from a subcultural perspective complements and supports Helmer's findings.[11] On one thing these more recent analyses agree: the essential ingredient in military organization is the degree to which the individual can be merged with the collectivity that is his military unit.

It is not surprising therefore that one of the theoretical themes which will provide a basis for this study is the degree to which men who commit absence offenses were capable of being integrated into the primary group networks which provide the foundation of effective military organization. As Edward Shils has noted, "The deserters from the armed forces of the United States in the period when they were engaged in the war in Indochina were much like the deserters from the United States Army in earlier wars, like deserters from the Wehrmacht in World War II and like deserters from the Soviet Army in Eastern Germany."[12] From this perspective, an individual's ability to become integrated into a military unit is related to the degree to which he was integrated into the civilian society.

What social background conditions might be associated with poor integration into civilian society? In contemporary American society, limited educational experience or intelligence which measures low on a standard scale are conditions which immediately come to mind. Individuals with only a few years of formal education have often not had adequate exposure to the school systems which constitute the first major force in socialization beyond the family. School is often the first secondary group in which the individual must create a primary group niche for himself, and those who for some reason do not undergo this transition into the world of secondary groups may remain socially handicapped for the rest of their lives. The finding of Stouffer and his colleagues that absence offenders were more likely than other offenders to have been truant from school as children is indicative of this phenomenon.[13]

In this study, measured intelligence is considered not as a biological condition but as a cultural one. To the extent that intelligence quotients can be used as an indicator of how well an individual is socialized into the society's dominant culture, then individuals who enter the military with low intelligence scores on standardized tests can be regarded as poorly integrated into the national culture and therefore less likely to be integrated into a military organization.

Members of racial minorities are less likely to be integrated into a dominant white culture; and in some cases, social integration into the ethnic community may further separate an individual from the dominant culture. For example, there is a good possibility that blacks by becoming integrated into primary group formations in the black community become collectively less integrated into the dominant white culture. As a result of such a situation, the experiences of black men in the Vietnam era require an especially careful analysis.

While this section has examined the question of desertion from the perspective of the system's needs and has basically asked why some individuals did not fit into that system, the following section will examine theories that propose structural contradictions within the military organization and sometimes society itself in explaining desertion and draft avoidance.

Social Conflict Themes

"I served two tours of duty in Vietnam! I gave three-quarters of my body for America, and what do I get? Spit in the face!", screamed paralyzed Marine Corps veteran Ron Kovic as his wheelchair was forcibly removed from the Republican National Convention in 1972.[14] Outside the convention hall and camped in nearby Flamingo Park were approximately 1,200 more Vietnam Veterans Against the War. It was an unprecedented event in American history. With the nation still engaged in war, some veterans of the war, honorably discharged, decorated, and sometimes maimed, were calling for victory by the other side and U.S. surrender.

The American armed forces in Vietnam were not the first to experience a crisis of morale while engaged with the enemy. However, there are many who find casualty levels and tangible strategic losses to be unsatisfactory explanations for the degree of disintegration which the American forces experienced in Indochina. As Lieutenant Colonel William Hauser, who labeled the war "the longest and most unpopular . . . in American history," phrased the question, "Are these crises the product of the Vietnam War, or did the conflict merely exacerbate and expose tensions and weaknesses already existing within the Army."[15]

In their study of disintegration and cohesion in the Wehrmacht during the last years of World War II, Shils and Janowitz found that external factors such as incompetency and corruption in their own political regime were not as responsible for the morale of the troops as internal factors such as relations between officers and men, primary relations among the men, and the social psychological relationship of the individual soldier to the military.[16] That the same conditions held in Vietnam is suggested by a War College study cited by Paul Savage and Richard Gabriel in their article "Cohesion and Disintegration in the American Army." Examining statistics on desertion, "fraggings," mutinies, and drug use in Vietnam, Savage and Gabriel argue that there was unambiguous evidence of "military internal decay verging on collapse" in the U.S. forces in Vietnam.[17]

Richard Boyle has written about several of the troop revolts which brought the American ground campaign to a halt in 1971, and Guenter Lewy has detailed the extent of such indices of social conflict as fraggings, mutinies, and substance abuse within the U.S. forces during the final years of the war.[18] As previously noted, John Helmer describes an American force that internally consisted of three drug-using subcultures based on alcohol, marijuana, and the opiates.[19] Even among highly motivated combat troops, Charles Moskos found motivation to be a function of certain "latent ideologies" as opposed to any specific understanding of national political goals.[20]

Three social-conflict or neo-Marxist theoretical concepts will be used to assist in deciphering the conflicts which characterized military service during the Second Indochina War. These are class, alienation, and social control. One thesis is that military service, especially as it occurred during the Vietnam era, was a class-based phenomenon. A second is that military participation can be characterized as a form of alienation. Third, it will be suggested that, given the two foregoing theses, military service can be understood as a problem of social control.

In the first part of his definition of a class, Max Weber describes it as "when a number of people have in common a specific causal component of their life chances." For Weber this component is formed "exclusively by economic interests" and must be "represented under the conditions of the commodity or labor markets."[21] Other more recent theorists have spoken of classes in terms of ownership and control. Since the definition of class is not an object of study here, only the most general application of the concept will be used. It is hoped that such general application will spare this work's being ensnarled in Marxian and anti-Marxian arguments. Since all that is available for constructing arguments about class in this book are already established criteria of education, one questionnaire item on subjective social class, and a number of other variables which might be taken as characteristics of poverty, class will be spoken of in terms of upper and lower.

Class will not be treated as a totally economic phenomenon, however. It is as much a cultural as an economic concept. Stanley Aronowitz in his *False Promises* has emphasized the ways that class is reflected in the consciousness of an individual member of a class.[22] In the situation of military service, where the individual confronts the state in a very asymmetric interaction, nothing may prove more important to the outcome of this interaction than the individual's image of self. A sense of powerlessness can be magnified to the nth degree in the face of the most powerful and the most legitimate of institutions.

Another aspect of the performance of military service hinges on the question of the nature of that service in terms of psychic fulfillment and self-actualization. Alienation is a condition which results from tension between the needs of an individual and the social relations which shape his existence.

The idea of an individual's interests being opposed to the goals of the organization of which he is a part is not a difficult one to grasp, especially in a military context. Every junior officer (and war-movie buff) knows that the conflict between "the mission" and "the needs of the men" is a continuing condition of military action. The connection of this definition of alienation to the more complex definition of alienation found in traditional Marxist literature requires some theoretical elaboration, and the resulting interpretation may not be acceptable to many Marxists.

The most concise statement of Karl Marx's theory of alienation is found in *The Economic and Philosophic Manuscripts of 1844.* Here, Marx focuses on the relationship between the propertyless worker and the product of his labor.

> This fact expresses merely that the object which labor produces — labor's product — confronts it as something alien, as a power independent of the producer. The product of labor is labor which has been enbodied in an object, which has become material: it is the objectification of labor. Labor's realization is its objectification. In the sphere of political economy this realization of labor appears as loss of realization for the workers; objectification as loss of the object and bondage to it; appropriation as estrangement, as alienation.[23]

Labor in a capitalist society involves, according to Marx, an individual selling to another his or her capacity to produce or "labor power." When this capacity, purchased by another, is carried out, the product of this bought labor is considered to be the property of the capitalist who initially purchased the worker's labor power. Since it is the system of property ownership which distinguishes the worker from the capitalist in the first place, the worker by adding to the sum total of private property through his labor had added to his own oppression. Hence the object of a human being's production, and consequently the act of production itself, becomes part of that system of private property which alienates the worker from the collective accomplishments of his species. With the greatest achievements of capitalist society embodied in the manifestations of private property, the worker is disassociated from the triumphs of his species, even though these triumphs are the result of the productive efforts of him and his fellow workers.

Alienation is above all, for Marx, the separation of the individual from his own productive efforts, which are in fact the badge of his humanity. According to Marx, only human beings produce "universally" by participating in a social process of production, and it is only by such participation that humans are distinguished from other animals.[24] In the process of alienation, a worker comes very naturally to view his productive efforts as belonging to another. As his own, the worker retains only his activities away from the workplace. "Therefore, the worker only feels himself freely active in his animal functions — eating, drinking, procreating, or at most in his dwelling and in his dressing up, etc.; and in his human functions, he no longer feels himself to be anything but an animal. What is animal becomes human and what is human becomes animal."[25]

Gerth and Mills in discussing Max Weber's writings on bureaucracy argue that according to the Weberian perspective of alienation, the alienation of the industrial worker is only one aspect of a more universal phenomenon. As an example, they suggest, "The modern soldier is equally 'separated' from the means of violence."[27]

The state, especially in parliamentary regimes with capitalist economies, can very appropriately be described as a product of human labor. The United States makes no denial of the origin of its state apparatus in an act of revolutionary violence. Without the military labor of those men and women who made the American Revolution, the state in America as an entity independent of foreign domination would not exist. It is possible to assert that this consolidation of the means of violence under the auspices of the new state constituted for the American ruling class a structural modification essential to its continued domination of the economic sphere. More importantly, this labor of military violence was fundamental to the maintenance of the state's existence and its expansion both economic and political.

The performance of this military labor can be easily described using the rubric of Marx's formulation of alienation. Just as a person is actualized as a human being through participation in the means of production, so is an individual a citizen by his potential to participate in the functioning of the state. The most radical form this participation takes is the performance of military service. As has already been suggested, the labor required to maintain the means of violence at the disposal of the state is necessary for the survival of the state and its associated economic base. The hallmarks of citizenry under a parliamentary regime are the individual freedoms and rights associated with the label of citizen. In providing the labor necessary for the actualization of the state, the citizen who becomes a military actor forgoes many of the individual freedoms associated with being a citizen. Under a different system of justice from his fellow citizens, the soldier loses even the limited freedom of the proletarian to sell his labor power on the open market.

It is his unique position within the jurisdiction of the system of military justice which negates the soldier's status as citizen. That the social fabric of military institutions, especially in war, is maintained by the threat of physical violence is argued by military theorists as diverse as Robert E. Lee[27] and Leon Trotsky.[28] Ironically, the potential violence which separates the soldier from his status as citizen is the same potential violence produced by the soldier's violence. Hence, the soldier, like the worker, is oppressed by the product of his own labor. Unlike the worker, he may not even be able to regard his natural (animal) functions as his own. It is as a soldier that he realizes his status as citizen—but it is also as a soldier that he loses those attributes which define him as citizen. What is noncitizen becomes citizen and what is citizen becomes noncitizen.

In a system in which alienation of participants is the rule, failure on the part of some individuals to meet institutional needs is inevitable. The problem for the institution becomes one of maintaining social control. An ideal process from the perspective of the institution would be one which treats the individual who chooses his own immediate need over those of the institution as a defective organizational component. He can be properly labeled and his punishment can be used as a negative example for other individuals who might be tempted to opt for personal as opposed to institutional needs in the future. The relationship between the functional and alienation approaches is very clear in this instance. By his attempt to serve self and his failure to do so, the deserter becomes functional to the institution by serving as an element in the social control of other alienated individuals.

It is important to emphasize that an individual who exists in a state of alienation will not necessarily fail to serve the needs of the institution which is responsible for that state, nor will his attitudes necessarily reflect his alienation. Even though there is an accentuated dependence on the violent aspects of social control in military institutions, such a focus obscures the essential internalized aspects of social control in any modern institution. In his *Social Control in the Welfare State,* Morris Janowitz stresses that the major mechanism of social control is the phenomenon of self-control.[29] Theorists from Durkheim to Habermas have emphasized that it is the moral or mental aspects which cement the social order into whatever stability that it may have.[30] This moves the discussion to the third theoretical perspective, which is concerned with the human person as decision maker.

A Theory of Purposive Action

An additional theoretical perspective which will prove useful to an analysis of avoidance and resistance behavior during the Second Indochina War is that which regards a human being as a goal-oriented actor attempting to maximize his gains in an institutionally constrained environment.[31] Just as the social integration and alienation perspectives do not each require the rejection of the other, this third approach is likewise compatible with the others. In *Power and the Structure of Society,* James Coleman suggests that a striking feature of the twentieth century is the existence of large corporate actors which through the complex processes of modern social organization and institutionalization take on an autonomy often beyond the control of individual actors. Just as Max Weber warned that bureaucracy might become an "iron cage" which imprisons its creators, Coleman suggests that these corporate actors increasingly confront individual actors as insensitive robot-like mechanisms bent on the single-minded pursuit of narrow interests.[32] From the perspective of the men who faced the Selective Service System and the armed forces personnel structure during the Vietnam War, these confrontations epitomized the sense of powerlessness which Coleman finds characteristic of individuals dealing with corporate actors.

It was impossible to become a military casualty of Vietnam if a man could avoid military service there. Baskir and Strauss outline the channeling mechanisms by which an individual could end up as a casualty of Vietnam or experience one of a number of other more desirable outcomes. If an individual is a purposive actor with an interest in avoiding military service or Vietnam, he can be expected to choose among courses of action which might allow him to achieve his own interest in opposition to that of the corporate actors which threaten his interest. In this way, the actor may be viewed as consciously or unconsciously faced with a series of strategy choices, and his fate as to a certain degree dependent on the effectiveness with which he utilizes these strategies.

An important consideration in this context is evidence that certain social categories of individuals are more capable than others of dealing with complex organizations. M. Brewster Smith in his review of the literature on social competence notes the class-based nature of the acquisition of social skills.[33] In *Class and Conformity,* Melvin Kohn found that working-class parents attempt to teach their children to be obedient and conforming, while middle class parents struggle to produce children who are autonomous and unafraid to manipulate their environment.[34] If this is the case, it can be expected that the higher the class status of an individual the more likely he is to succeed in achieving his interest through strategic maneuvering against a corporate actor.

Some evidence for this perspective already exists in the discrepancies in the probability of casualties across various social categories. An analysis of Korean Conflict casualties for the city of Detroit conducted by Albert J. Mayer and Thomas F. Hoult revealed higher casualty rates for predominantly black census tracts.[35] Comparing Wisconsin's Vietnam casualties to a sample of high school seniors allowed Maurice Zeitlin, Kenneth Lutterman, and James Russell to conclude that men from poor families and men who were sons of workers were overrepresented among casualties.[36] In a study of 101 Cook County communities, Badillo and Curry found the socioeconomic status of the community to be more important in predicting the Vietnam casualties suffered by the community than was the community's racial composition.[37] Their findings led them to suggest that blacks, rather than being victims of overt racial discrimination in military personnel policy, were victims of the same bureaucratic conscription and assignment procedures which made poor whites more likely to become casualties. Evidence to be presented in this book will make it possible to test this kind of assertion.

2

Foundations

Lawrence Baskir and William Strauss began the work which this book continues in their books *Reconciliation After Vietnam* and *Chance and Circumstance*.[1] This chapter will first summarize the more significant of their findings and suggest reasons why a third book is necessary. Next it will describe the two data sets upon which the findings and conclusions which follow are based. This will be followed by a brief social demographic description of draft offenders and military absence offenders.

Baskir and Strauss

Baskir and Strauss are lawyers, and their two books are a lawyer's view of what happened to the generation who faced military service under the system of conscription used during the Second Indochina War. Both men served as key members of the legal staff of President Ford's Clemency Board. From their firsthand knowledge, they describe the origins and workings of this board, which, despite its many official limitations and inadvertent shortcomings, they feel to have been a more successful effort in behalf of "bad paper" veterans than any subsequent measure by the Carter administration. The Ford Clemency Board reached nineteen percent of its target population, while the Carter administration's discharge upgrade project affected only nine percent of those whom it might have benefited. Baskir and Strauss show how both programs suffered at the hands of strong opponents ironically placed in important program roles and from the actions of a hostile Congress.

Included in *Reconciliation After Vietnam* is the authors' proposal for alleviating the situations of veterans with less-than-honorable discharges while preserving the integrity of a nation which may be facing an era of defense unreadiness. As they note in *Chance and Circumstance,* their suggestions for repatriating draft offenders were, of course, outdated by President Carter's blanket pardon.

Throughout both books is a continued concern with the widespread public ignorance about the population of men who are the focus of the amnesty debate. Instead of the singleminded, politically outspoken dissidents portrayed by both the American left and the American Legion, Baskir and Strauss reveal a diversified cross section of an American generation. All too many of these men come from the lower strata of the working class. Images of vocal rebels in Canada and Sweden are statistically overshadowed by a mass of urban minority members and impoverished Southerners.

The analyses of Baskir and Strauss are not restricted to the labeled portions of the Vietnam generation. They are just as interested in profiling the "artful dodgers" who effectively manipulated the Selective Service System, the men who just hoped they would be overlooked and were just missed, the men who used safer branches of service as a haven from the threat of Vietnam, and the disenchanted veterans with honorable discharges. With nearly forgotten phrases such as "shake and bakes" and "getting your ticket punched,"[2] they present through their careful review of the literature and personal research the gamut of ways in which a generation coped with an unpopular war.

Though Pentagon officials have claimed that the rate of Vietnam-era absence offenses was no higher than that of World War II or the Korean War, Baskir and Strauss detail a number of differences which distinguish the absence offenders of the Second Indochina War from their counterparts in previous wars. First, the overall rate for the Second Indochina War is very deceptive, as is revealed in a year-by-year breakdown of absence statistics. Desertion rates for this last war started relatively low and climbed geometrically as the war continued (see Table 2-1). Just as other authors have done previously, Baskir and Strauss associate this pattern with the nearly-identical pattern of growing hostility toward the war among the American public.[3]

There are, however, some additional and more obvious factors related to this delayed increase in Second Indochina War desertions. It wasn't until August 1966 that Secretary of Defense Robert McNamara announced the launching of Project 100,000, the program which would attempt to salvage hundreds of thousands of young men from economic deprivation by bringing them into the armed services.[4] Inducted, for the most part, into the Army and Marines, these men would come to be overrepresented in both the population of deserters and Indochina combat units. "McNamara's boys" or the "moron corps,"[5] as they were sometimes called by command-

Table 2-1.   **Desertion Rates for**
                    Recent U. S. Military Involvements

War	Year	Desertions per 1000 Active Duty Personnel
World War II	1944	63
	1945	45
Korean War	1951	14
	1952	22
	1953	22
	1954	16
Second Indochina War	1965	16
	1966	15
	1967	21
	1968	29
	1969	42
	1970	52
	1971	73

Source: Office of Defense Secretary, cited in "An Interview with Walter Collins," *Southern Exposure* 1 (1973): 14.

ers, would have been excluded from military service as mentally unquali-fied at any time before or after President Johnson's dramatic escalation of American troop strength in Vietnam. These Category IV soldiers[6] were three times as likely to desert from basic training, two times as likely to not complete their tours, and two-and-a-half times more likely to be court-martialed as other soldiers.

Another large group of deserters noted by Baskir and Strauss are those men who served in Vietnam and deserted *after* completing their tours when assigned to stateside duty. An estimated twenty thousand Vietnam veter-ans received less-than-honorable discharges for absence offenses which were committed between return to stateside and termination of service.[7] As in the case of Project 100,000 inductees, Vietnam veteran "short-timer" deser-tion was a phenomenon which must be structurally related to the dragging on of American involvement.

Baskir and Strauss emphasize that, by historical standards, combat-related desertions were very rare in Vietnam. Yet, periods of absence asso-ciated with desertion did become increasingly longer in the later years of the war. Given the climate of heightened drug abuse and racial tension in the armed forces, Baskir and Strauss use their legal experience to argue that military justice became especially arbitrary, with little or no variations in type of offense associated with the assignment of the precisely ordered grades of military discharges to offenders.

Baskir and Strauss take materials from a variety of sources to produce a thorough review of the literature. The full worth of this painstaking exercise cannot be conveyed in any summary, and to those who find the present work of any use, their two books are highly recommended. There are, however, limitations to their methods of analysis which provide the necessity for this further examination of their data. It must be noted that all of what they have found and much of what they suggest is confirmed in what follows.

Using percentages and case studies, Baskir and Strauss demonstrate that a great deal of social injustice characterized service and sacrifice in the Second Indochina War. Yet, in all but a few cases, their method of analysis is limited to looking at one variable at a time. For example, they show that a certain percentage of men got married in hopes of avoiding the draft. This is a very interesting social fact, but since Baskir and Strauss gathered a great deal of additional information on these men, a further statistical analysis of their data reveals a more complex social picture. Relationships between this variable, and other variables can be especially important. It is not surprising that men who got married to avoid the draft were more likely to have children to avoid the draft. But it is interesting that men who got married to avoid the draft were not significantly more likely than others to attempt late registration as a means of escaping conscription. And it is interesting that pursuing marriage as a draft avoidance strategy is, statistically speaking, mildly related to being from a lower social class background. What may be most important, though, is what was totally invisible to Baskir and Strauss's method of analysis: men who got married to avoid conscription were not significantly less likely to perform military service.

Most of what follows is an extension of the work of Baskir and Strauss. This will be accomplished by examining the relationships among the variables used in their studies of the Presidential Clemency Board data and the data generated by the Notre Dame Survey of the Vietnam Generation.

Presidential Clemency Board Data

President Ford issued an executive order establishing a clemency program for Vietnam-era draft and military absence offenders on September 16, 1974. By the end of this program, 21,800 of the 27,000 individuals who had applied for this program had been ruled eligible for the program's benefits.[8] What is referred to in the following pages as the Presidential Clemency Board (PCB) data set is in fact a 1,481-case stratified random sample of clemency board applicants taken from the official files which are stored at the Center for Civil Rights at the University of Notre Dame. Since the clemency board dealt with both civilian and military offenders, who have been shown to represent considerably differing populations, the sample was stratified according to the applicant's military status at the time of the offense. The result is a sample of 472 civilian offenders and 1,009 veterans.

Since the Presidential Clemency Board data constitutes a sample of the clemency program applicants and not of the total population of individuals who might be eligible for amnesty, it is important to make certain qualifications. The first such qualification is that the parameters of the total population eligible for some sort of amnesty for illegal activities with respect to the Second Indochina War are unknown. The only estimate of the number of individuals who did not register for the draft, who constitute only a portion of the Vietnam offenders, is the one which was used by President Carter and was provided by Baskir and Strauss from the Notre Dame Survey of the Vietnam Generation (to be discussed next). In addition, all such estimates hinge on the diverse definitions of the amnesty-eligible population.

Second, following from this, certain individuals who are often thought of as being within an amnesty-eligible population were consciously excluded from the Ford program. Clearly directed not to apply to the Ford program were military personnel who had been convicted of other-than-absence-related offenses. Any military individual who refused a direct order as a result of objection to the war, and did not desert in connection with that refusal, is not included in this sample. The number of antiwar activists who were arrested for obstructing the Selective Service process were excluded from the Ford program and therefore are not represented by this sample. Also in this category are all draft-card burners and the man in North Carolina who was imprisoned for using obscenities in public to describe the war. Finally, all the individuals who were eligible for the Ford Clemency program and did not apply could not be included in the sample. Since the Clemency Board itself estimated that 113,300 persons were eligible for its program, a considerable number of eligible nonapplicants are involved. Of more specific concern here is how the nonconsideration of the nonapplicants might bias the sample. In Table 2-2, the Clemency Board Report estimated the percentages of nonapplication for each group eligible for clemency. Though the degree of nonapplication was high across the board, it is interesting to note that it was highest for the largest category, those military personnel who received undesirable discharges as a result of absence offenses. In suggesting reasons for nonapplication, the Clemency Board listed an unawareness of the program and its offering, on the one hand, and on the other, an unwillingness to lose settled statuses in communities and jobs. Despite the high rate of nonapplication, the Defense

Table 2-2.   **Degree of Nonapplication to Ford Clemency Board
                  By Selected Categories (PCB)**

Category	Estimated N	Estimated Percent Not Applying
Convicted civilians	8,700	78
Unconvicted civilians	4,522	84
Convicted military bad conduct/ dishonorable discharge	24,872	78
Undesirable discharge	65,517	87

Department with its access to the records of applicants and nonapplicants alike was able to declare that the two groups were similar with respect to a number of factors such as Armed Forces Qualifying Test (AFQT) scores, education, family background, type of offense, and circumstances of offense.[9]

Survey of the Vietnam Generation

In 1975, Baskir and Strauss, with the assistance of a staff assembled at the Notre Dame Center for Civil Rights, conducted a survey of the generation of males who were eligible for the draft during the Second Indochina War. To obtain a sample of any specialized subset of the general population can be very difficult. Given limited financial resources and a population for whom no accurate listing is available, the only feasible approach is what Seymour Sudman has labeled random sampling with quotas. To as great a degree as possible, Baskir and Strauss approximated this method.

In random sampling with quotas, the reseachers must first select geographic areas to be sampled. These geographic areas must then be broken down into subunits based on some known characteristic such as population distribution, racial composition, or socioeconomic status. Each interviewer is then sent to some randomly-selected location within the geographic subunit. From this randomly-selected starting point, the interviewer moves in a randomly-selected direction proceeding from dwelling to dwelling until a previously designated number of respondents who are members of the population under study are found. In order to insure that certain subgroups within the population are included in the sample in adequate numbers, the interviewers may be given specific breakdowns in their quotas of respondents who must possess the certain attribute.[10]

An important consideration in taking such a sample is to insure the maximum variation in the geographic areas included. Given their available resources, Baskir and Strauss did this by selecting three very different American cities. Very convenient to the Center for Civil Rights was the city of South Bend, Indiana, a midwestern city of moderate size located in a politically conservative agricultural region and having a relatively small nonresident student population. Not as convenient, yet still accessible, was Ann Arbor, Michigan. The scene of much antiwar activity, Ann Arbor is in a very urban region and has a large resident student population. In contrast to South Bend and Ann Arbor, which are predominantly white, was Baskir and Strauss' third city, Washington, D.C., with its predominantly black population.

Carefully selecting census tracts of varying socioeconomic and ethnic compositions, Baskir and Strauss assigned the members of their staff quotas according to race and veterans' status. Since their staff did not consist of professional interviewers, Baskir and Strauss concentrated on the design of the questionnaire itself. As respondents were expected to give what would sometimes be self-incriminating answers to some items, much emphasis was placed on the Center for Civil Rights and the University of Notre Dame's responsibility for the anonymity of the respondents. It was hoped that the reputation for integrity of these two institutions would encourage these men to answer the questions honestly and completely. In order to further extend a sense of privacy, questionnaires were left with respondents and arrangements were made for picking them up at a later time.

The result of this effort is a sample of 1,566 American males who were born after July 1939 and before April 1955. Although in this book it may sometimes sound as if the Notre Dame survey is being treated as a sample of the entire Vietnam generation, the author is well aware that it is not. Most conspicuously absent from its ranks are the men of the rural South, with their disproportionate ratio of military participation and their distinctive traditions of military service. Despite the absence of these men and of men from other regions of the country from this sample, the Notre Dame survey, at this time, constitutes the largest, and perhaps the only, data set of its kind. It can be a source of much understanding about the men who faced the peculiar choices of the Vietnam generation.

The Social Demography of the Vietnam Offender[11]

Using the Presidential Clemency Board data set, the following sections will attempt to describe the population of men who have been the focus of the amnesty debate. As has been often noted, these men constitute two separate populations of offenders. On the one hand are the civilian draft offenders, a cross section of American youth distinguished only by their tendency toward ideological and moral motivations. On the other hand stand the military absence offenders, members of the lowest strata of the American class structure. Since President Carter eliminated the amnesty debate with respect to the draft-avoider portion of the sample, the major share of attention will be devoted to the population of military offenders.

The Civilian Offenders

Perhaps the most surprising statistic with respect to the amnesty issue is the size of the two populations of individuals involved. Previously most debate had centered on the approximately thirteen-thousand civilian offenders, with little public interest in the approximately one-hundred-thousand military offenders, despite the fact that the latter population is, in terms of labeled offenders, at least seven times larger. Though it is the latter group which remains the greater mystery for most Americans, some of the information on the draft-avoider stratum of the Clemency Board data may bear examining.

Two groups of religious objectors figure importantly among the convicted civilians. Making up twenty-one percent of the civilian offenders in the Clemency Board sample, Jehovah's Witnesses were forbidden by their religious beliefs to serve their country in the Conscientious Objector (CO) status available to members of other faiths. In a different situation were the Black Muslims (a much smaller percentage of the civilians), whose religion led them to object to only the Second Indochina War as differentiated from war in general. It is the presence of this large number of religious objectors which brings into some question the stereotype most of us have of the upper-middle class, philosophically and verbally eloquent draft resister who fled to Canada or Scandinavia.

Overall, the civilians in the Clemency Board sample appear to be very similar to all the young men in their cohort. Eighty-seven percent of them are white, while the proportions of black (11 percent) and Spanish-speaking (1.3 percent) are about the same as those of the general population. Seventy-nine percent have at least a high school diploma and eighteen percent are college graduates. Twenty-nine percent come from economically-disadvantaged backgrounds and most, sixty-nine percent, grew up in two-parent homes.

There is, however, one large disproportionality evident among the civilian offenders. There are comparatively few Southerners, while Westerners, particularly from the Pacific Coast, are overrepresented (over one-fourth of the sample). This is not surprising if previous studies of Selective Service and judicial practices are considered.[12]

Service Careers of Military Offenders

An examination of the service careers of the military offenders yields some surprising findings. Of the one-thousand and nine military offenders in the sample, twenty-seven percent served in Vietnam. One percent of the total went AWOL while in the combat zone, and two percent did so while on R and R (rest and relaxation leave, usually in Bangkok, Hong Kong, Australia, or Honolulu) or on leave. In the case of these individuals, the charge, often cited by politicians, that some other individual had to take their place holds true; but for the twenty-four percent of all absentee offenders who honorably completed their Vietnam tours, this charge is not appropriate. Of these twenty-four percent, all but one percent of the total deserted shortly *after* reassignment to a stateside base. Of the total group of military offenders, 3.5 percent were wounded in action in Vietnam. In all of these cases of immediate post-Vietnam desertion, Ford's Clemency Board in its case-by-case review attributed the act of desertion to combat fatigue or some aspect of Post-Vietnam Syndrome.[13]

Eighty-four percent of the military offenders in the sample had enlisted for military service. All but 19.2 percent had served for more than six months and 29 percent had more than the two years honorable service, which is all that would have been required of them had they been drafted. One third of these military offenders had enlisted prior to their eighteenth birthdays.

Absence offenses during the Vietnam era were not uniform across branches of service. As can be seen in Table 2-3, disproportionately few in this sample of military offenders come from the more technical and prestigious branches of service, the Navy and the Air Force. In the Army and Marine Corps, the branches of service which bore the brunt of the ground fighting and casualties throughout most of the war, the reverse is true.

Social Class Background of Offenders

A number of the pardoned draft resisters who were interviewed on television following Carter's pardon made statements concerning the social class difference between draft resisters and military offenders. Evidence that undermines some widespread beliefs about the upper and upper-middle class background of draft avoiders has already been noted; there is also

Table 2-3.	Comparison of Branch of Service Breakdowns for Absence Offenders and Total Armed Forces[14]	
Branch of Service	Percent of Total 1970 Military Personnel	Percent of Absence Offenders
Air Force	25.8	3.0
Navy	22.6	11.6
Army	43.1	62.3
Marine Corps	8.5	23.0

much evidence that military offenders are from the lower, poorly educated strata of American society.

First, it is again important to call the reader's attention to a military program unique to the late sixties. Prior to the Second Indochina War, it had become government policy to limit acceptance or conscription for military service of individuals who scored within category IV on the Armed Forces Qualifying Test (below the thirtieth percentile or below 80 on most standard IQ tests). Despite the low level of mobilization necessary for the initial invasion of Vietnam, a manpower shortage especially in the combat arms developed. In August 1966, Secretary of Defense Robert McNamara announced Project 100,000, which would not only assist in meeting manpower needs, but would also "use the training establishment of Armed Forces to help certain young men become more productive citizens upon return to civilian life." The "opportunity and obligation of military service" was extended to "marginally qualified" persons.[15] Men scoring as low as ten percent on the AFQT (IQ approximately equal 60) could then enlist or be drafted into the armed services. During the three years before it was discontinued, Project 100,000 brought 240,000 of these "marginally qualified" persons onto active duty. *At least one third of this sample of military offenders entered active duty under the auspices of this program.*

Once again region plays an important factor in the geographic distribution of offender origins. This time it is the South which is overrepresented in the sample, with approximately eighteen percent of all military offenders coming from the Fifth Circuit Court District (six Deep South states) alone.

While the educational levels of civilian offenders approximated the national estimate of eighty percent graduating from high school, the educational levels of military offenders were considerably lower. Over three-quarters of the military offenders have not completed high school. Twenty-one percent were black and 3.5 percent were Spanish-speaking, well above the national population parameters for these groups. Sixty percent were from broken homes with one or both natural parents absent throughout most of childhood, and 74.7 percent came from homes classified by federal income guidelines as economically unstable.

The Ford Clemency Board tended to offer clemency more readily to individuals who were able to state moral or political objections to the war in Vietnam. Among the military offenders, less than five percent mention such objections when asked about their motivation in committing their absence offense. Substantially more than that, as previously mentioned, deserted in objection to military life on stateside posts after returning from Vietnam.

The Clemency Board, and President Carter, showed less willingness to grant clemency to individuals (1) who violated an oath to their country and (2) who were motivated in their offense by "selfish" reasons. All the military offenders very clearly fall into the first category and most of them also fall into the second. Seven percent of them deserted upon the receipt of orders for Vietnam. A feeling that the military had subjected them to procedural irregularities or outright deception in its assignment processes was given as an excuse for desertion by 8.6 percent. Others, however, mentioned factors related to their social origins including marital problems (8.4 percent) and financial burdens placed on family obligations by being in military service (32.7).

It is important before proceeding in this analysis to recall Baskir and Strauss's dismay at the gap between the public myths about the Vietnam era deserter and the social reality. Their research and the material included in this chapter do not produce an image of the Vietnam offender compatible with the more glamorous portrayals all too commonly favored by the media as well as by social activists of diverse political perspectives. Deserter status does not necessarily mean that a man was spared the experience of service in Indochina. Outspoken, ideologically astute resisters of American imperialism are as common to the evening news as they are uncommon to the population of Vietnam offenders. Members of minorities and individuals born in the lowest strata of the American social structure are overrepresented among offenders. The mechanics of how all these men came to be labeled as "deserters" will be the subject of the chapters which follow. With the aid of the theoretical perspectives in Chapter One, it is hoped that morality play will give way to an understanding of social process.

3

Dynamics of Desertion:
Crime and Punishment

Desertion is a military crime that has no civilian equivalent in American society. A soldier is considered absent-without-leave if he is missing from his military unit for any period of time, though he is usually not reported as such unless one full day has elapsed. If he is absent-without-leave for more than thirty days, he is administratively classified as a deserter. Under the Uniform Code of Military Justice, a man cannot be legally convicted of desertion unless a court-martial proves that he had no intention of returning to his unit.[1] In more common usage, a soldier who abandons his unit for any period of time is called a deserter. Here, unless it is specifically noted, desertion will always be used in this common way as an interchangeable term for absence offense.

Most of the research that has been done on the men who deserted during the Second Indochina War has used the data gathered by the Presidential Clemency Board.[2] One shortcoming of this procedure is that there is little chance to compare deserters with nondeserters or men who were absent-without-leave and labeled as such with men who were absent-without-leave but never officially labeled. Since the Notre Dame survey asked its veteran respondents about AWOL infractions, some such comparisons can now be made.

Social Background of Absence Offenders

The social background of men who go AWOL is a very important issue in all three of the major theoretical perspectives referred to above. From the functional point of view, certain social types just don't make good soldiers. These social types often consist of the same individuals who have

25

trouble succeeding in civilian society. Under the purposive actor model of behavior, an individual has a certain degree of power over his environment through his choices of actions. If it is assumed that going AWOL is inefficient strategy for coping with the demands of military life, then such behavior is likely to be pursued by individuals already lacking in social competence. From another perspective, if most soldiers exist in some degree of alienation and the military needs some deserters to serve as examples in a process of social control, then it could be argued that the best examples would be the soldiers who were considered of least worth to the organization in the first place.

The work of Stouffer and his associates in the Second World War[3] and the research of Baskir and Strauss[4] and Bell and Houston[5] on Vietnam deserters have all suggested that those who commit absence offenses are more likely to come from lower class backgrounds. This will be the first question considered in comparing deserters with other servicemen in the Notre Dame sample.

Men who answered "yes" to a question concerning whether they had gone AWOL even for a short period of time were significantly more likely to be black (3-1).* This coincides with the finding that blacks and other minorities are overrepresented in the Clemency Board data. It also fits the descriptions of exacerbated racial tensions within the armed forces during the Vietnam era. Black soldiers who were being exposed to a growing movement of black nationalism and ethnic pride were faced with a generation of white officers whose own working class backgrounds made them particularly sensitive to any threat to discipline. Flight from duty may be considered one of the milder forms of rebellion in a period of fragging incidents and collective insubordination.

Perceived social class origin and level of educational attainment are also revealed to be significantly associated with going AWOL. Men in the sample who did not grow up in a home where both natural parents were present are likewise more apt to have gone AWOL during their tour of active duty (3-1).

The three factors — race, class, and family structure — unite to show the class nature of going AWOL as a response to military service. A man's lower class origin makes him less likely to experience the socializing experiences of the family and the schools and more likely to go AWOL when on active

---

*The majority of the statistical tables upon which the text is based have been placed in an appendix. When a statement is made on the basis of a particular table, the number of that table is referred to in parentheses.

duty in the armed services. This concurs perfectly with the studies on World War II soldiers. It also indicates that the findings of the Notre Dame survey are in agreement with other research which has shown the Vietnam era deserter more likely to have been the product of a lower class family and of fewer years of formal education.

Several studies of the military involvement in Southeast Asia have contended that desertions became more frequent as hostility to the war among the American public increased.[6] The Notre Dame survey reinforces this view, since the younger the veteran in the sample, the more likely he is to have gone AWOL.

Shils and Janowitz argued that World War II desertions were seldom associated with identifiable ideological perspectives.[7] In contrast, right-wing critics of the American military's performance during the Second Indochina War have argued that much of the American soldier's problem was a state of mind. Others have turned on the whole Vietnam generation as being pampered by their parents and devoid of schooling in the traditions of patriotism.[8] Three variables which relate to this part of the Vietnam debate are whether the respondent's father had served in the military, how his parents felt about conscription, and how the young man himself felt about the war when he was of draft eligible age. In the sample obtained in the Notre Dame survey, none of these three factors show any relationship with a man's going AWOL (3-1). This data indicates that neither the ideological milieu of the family nor an individual's opinion of the war played a determining role in the overall phenomenon of Vietnam-era desertion.

With respect to the theoretical possibility that military service during the Second Indochina War alienated a majority of its possible participants and the theory that desertion was just a poor strategy among many for coping with military service, an additional condition becomes important. Were the men who deserted also more likely to be among those who attempted to avoid the draft? The answer is no. Not only were young men who had attempted to avoid the draft before service not any more likely to desert; they were somewhat less likely to do so (3-1).

The Military Context of AWOL Offenses

The Presidential Clemency Board unearthed a number of unexpected facts about the military careers of Vietnam-era absence offenders. Over eighty percent of those who were discharged for such offenses had enlisted for military service. Almost one-third had entered active duty under Project 100,000. Almost a quarter of discharged absence offenders had actually served in Vietnam. A few had received wounds in action or decorations for valor.[9]

A breakdown according to type of induction for those veterans of military service included in the Notre Dame survey is displayed in Table 3-2. In this sample, there are as many men who enlisted to avoid the draft as there are genuine volunteers. Still, there is a positive relationship between being drafted and having gone AWOL at some time while on active duty (3-3). From the Presidential Clemency Board finding that a majority of veterans with less-than-honorable discharges had been volunteers,[10] it might have been expected that draftees with their shorter terms of mandatory service would have been less likely to go AWOL. The fact that the situation is reversed in the Notre Dame sample will have to be dealt with later in this chapter.

Total time spent on active duty bears no significant relationship to whether a man had ever gone AWOL, but how time on active duty was spent does. Men who served in Vietnam were significantly more likely to have gone AWOL while on active duty; and among only those men who served in Vietnam, those who experienced combat were significantly more likely to have gone AWOL at some point in their military careers (3-3).

These findings from the Notre Dame survey support one of the darkest suggestions of Baskir and Strauss in *Chance and Circumstance*.[11] Men who were exposed to Vietnam service were prone to commit absence offenses. The more radical their exposure, for example combat as opposed to noncombat, the more likely was the possibility of an absence offense. Since very few American servicemen deserted while assigned to Vietnam, a conceivable scenario presents itself. The veteran of Vietnam service is angered by the strains of stateside duty. After what he has seen, the day-to-day discipline of armed service life seems no longer worthy of his respect. He is confused and simply cannot adjust to any sort of routine after his experiences in the "unreal" world of Vietnam.[12] Though going AWOL is a condition peculiar to return to stateside military life, there is just as much chance that these stresses could have held for the veteran returning to a civilian job or to college.

In a later chapter, the phenomenon of manipulating the military personnel structure as a strategy of coping with military service is examined. At this point, it is important to note that there is no significant relationship between going AWOL and aggressively exercising the legal personnel options which might have given an individual soldier some control over his destiny (3-3).

Table 3-2.   Mode of Induction
                    into Armed Forces (NDS)

	Frequency	Percentage
Drafted	170	30.5
Enlisted to avoid conscription	194	34.6
Enlisted because wanted to	195	34.9
TOTAL	569	100.0

Patterns of Absence Offenses

The Presidential Clemency Board sample includes only men who received less-than-honorable discharges for their absence offenses, while the Notre Dame sample includes veterans who never went AWOL at all, men who did not receive less-than-honorable discharges for their absence offenses, and men who might have been eligible for the Clemency Board sample. Hence, comparison of the two samples is difficult and, in some cases, impossible. Nonetheless, an attempt will be made in this section to use findings from both samples to expand knowledge of the nature of absence offenses during the Second Indochina War. From the two data sets, it is possible to suggest what kinds of men committed what kinds of absence offenses. Variables are available for number of offenses, length of longest absence, and total months absent over a service career. Differences in findings between the two data sets will be noted, but explanations will be offered for such differences only when an explanation is feasible.

Blacks, who have been shown to be more likely to have gone AWOL, also report going AWOL a greater number of times. While their longest absence was usually not significantly longer than that of whites, their total months absent while on active duty is greater (3-1, 3-4, 3-5).

It is one thing to go AWOL. It is another to stay AWOL. In the smaller Notre Dame sample, number of times absent-without-leave is somewhat positively related to the longest period that a man was AWOL at any one time (3-6). In the larger PCB sample, times charged with being AWOL is negatively related to total months AWOL (3-7). A number of conditions could have been responsible for these outcomes, especially when it is recalled that four different variables in two different data sets are involved in these relationships. For one group of men, number of reported AWOLs, whether officially noted or not, is related to longest single absence. For the other group, officially recorded AWOLs are negatively related to total months absent. One explanation is that some might have been more socially competent at staying absent-without-leave than others.

There is additional evidence to support the hypothesis that certain socially defined categories of men were less effective at staying AWOL. While
men from the lower social strata were much more likely to go AWOL a
greater number of times, they did not stay AWOL for longer periods of
time (3-1). Among the bad-paper veterans in the Clemency Board data (who
are overwhelmingly from more deprived backgrounds), this results in a
greater number of AWOL attempts being associated with less total time
spent away from active duty.

This condition of not being very adept at staying AWOL may also explain a similar set of relationships for draftees and for soldiers with fewer
years of education. It also exactly fits the previously cited description of
absences among black veterans. Two other groups of veterans who follow
this pattern are those who served in Vietnam and those who experienced
combat there (3-3, 3-6, 3-7). Of course, a factor contributing to these men
being ineffective deserters was that they just didn't try to get away with
it. Almost nine out of ten of those absence offenders seen by the Presidential Clemency Board had made no attempt to hide while they were AWOL.[13]

On the other hand, the data indicates that there is also a correlation between the ability to remain absent without leave for relatively long periods
of time and recognized measures of social competency. For instance, there
is a mild relationship between AFQT category and longer periods of absence (3-7). Men who had originally postponed their entrance onto active
duty through some legal means and men who had attempted to find personnel structure loopholes to escape being assigned to Vietnam were less
likely to desert, but in the cases when they did, their time of absence from
active duty was significantly longer (3-1, 3-6). Other men with longer periods of absence include those who were older when they began active duty
and those who were able to secure civilian jobs while AWOL (3-7).

From the purposive actor point of view, there are two groups of men
who chose a bad strategy for coping with military service and deserted.
One of these groups, composed of individuals more likely to be black,
drafted, lower class, or with fewer years of education, either did not try
or were unable to maintain this strategy for very long. The other group
includes men who have characteristics not generally associated with deserting, such as slightly superior measured intelligence, greater maturity, and
experience at dealing with bureaucratic mechanisms. Evidence indicates
that this latter group was able to maintain their AWOL status for a longer
period of time.

The first of these groups can be divided one more time into those who
went AWOL many times and through repetitions of the offense built up

a considerable amount of total time absent-without-leave, and those who went AWOL many times and did not build up a large number of total months AWOL. In the first group are blacks and draftees; in the second, Vietnam veterans and the lower class whites with the least years of education. The veterans and lower class whites constitute either the least competent deserters or the most aimless.

The frequently encountered statistic that desertion became an increasingly worse problem as the Second Indochina War progressed is again reinforced by the Notre Dame sample and the Presidential Clemency Board data. The younger members of both samples who would have faced the last few years of the Vietnam involvement deserted more often and for longer periods of time than their older counterparts.

Baskir and Strauss emphasized the poverty which sometimes faced the enlisted men of the Vietnam generation.[14] Father Theodore Hesburgh focused his concern on the men who bore the burden of families to support under the conditions of military service during the Second Indochina War.[15] In a final note on the patterns of absence offenses during the war, married men deserted more frequently and for longer periods of time than did single men.[16]

Military Justice and the Absence Offender:
the Notre Dame Sample

It is very difficult to consider the fate of absence offenders without giving some attention to the legal system that classified them as offenders. Robert Sherrill's *Military Justice is to Justice as Military Music is to Music* through a series of case studies and an analytical review effectively attacks the Uniform Code of Military Justice and the conduct of military justice procedures.[17] Baskir and Strauss describe how the military justice system became overloaded at the end of the war. Under the pressure of increasing violations, they argue, the practice of military justice became erratic and inconsistent. Court-martial proceedings continued to be held, but the widespread and indiscriminant dispensing of Chapter 10 undesirable discharges did not insure that offenders received uniform treatment.[18]

In this section, an input-output analysis will be used to assess the fairness of the military justice system. The social background characteristics, conditions of military service, and conditions of offense will be considered input variables, and the severity of punishment will be considered the output variable. If the system operated fairly, it would seem that in most cases the social background and conditions of service variables should not be related to punishment outcomes, while aspects of the offense should be.

Since the question item related to severity of punishment in the Notre Dame survey is less suitable for quantitative analysis and the sample of offenders is smaller, it will be examined first.

Again the older portion of the Vietnam generation fared differently from those who were eligible for service later in the war. Severity of punishment was significantly greater for the older absence offenders in the sample. This is especially interesting because the most severe punishment option listed in the survey is being court-martialed. What this means is that early in the war, when there were not as many men going AWOL and the court-martial dockets were less full, a man was more likely to be court-martialed for an absence offense. Later in the war, with more absence offenses taking place, he was less likely to be court-martialed. Getting away with going AWOL was less likely before greater resistance to the war developed.

As it is worded, this variable is more an indicator of how a commander reacted to an absence offense than how a court-martial reacted to an offense. Commanders were no more likely to punish nonwhites, individuals from lower social strata, or draftees than other G.I.'s. Men with fewer years of education were, however, prone to draw stiffer reactions from commanders. A man's education may have given him a certain institutional or interpersonal expertise or an aura of potential for rehabilitation. The ability to verbalize one's perspective can prove invaluable in many social situations. Whatever the case, the higher a man's education the lower were his chances of receiving a tougher punishment for an absence offense.

There is a respect for experience which can be found in any occupation, and this is also the case in the profession of arms. It is not surprising, therefore, that men with greater time in service who committed an absence offense generally received less harsh punishment from their commanders than those with less time in service (3-8). Whether this was the result of the actions of the individual in successfully managing his absence or of the discretion of the commander is difficult to say. In the interactive situation that constitutes a military unit, it probably involves some degree of both.

The dialectical complications of analyzing social interaction mark the boundaries of quantitative analysis. From the data used here it is difficult to imagine the circumstances that contributed to a commander's decision to punish or not to punish, or to speculate on the factors which he used to determine the gravity of such punishment. Men who had attempted to avoid the draft were less likely in general to go AWOL once on active duty, but when they did and were caught, they were more likely to receive a more severe punishment from their commanders. Perhaps an occasional outspokenness or an enhanced sense of desperation accompanied these unsuccessful draft avoiders into the military justice process.

Contradicting somewhat the statistical correlation between severity of punishment and time in service is the lack of any indication that Vietnam service in any way mitigated a commander's decision to assign punishment to an AWOL soldier. Vietnam veterans, especially those with combat experience, were among the men most likely to go AWOL, yet, in the process of punishment their previous baptism by fire earned them few special favors (3-8). The degree to which Vietnam veterans did get certain kinds of "breaks" is discussed in Chapter Five.

Among those criteria which might be expected to have a strong effect on the commander's assessment of punishment, the Notre Dame survey variables on times absent without leave and length of longest absence would seem to be especially important. This is indeed the case for length of longest absence in that commanders were apt to respond more sternly to longer absences. The significance of the relationship between length of absence and degree of punishment is not matched by any similar relationship between the number of a man's absence offenses and the degree of his punishment (3-8).

Despite a concern in the Uniform Code of Military Justice with aggravating conditions in the administration of punishment, this data indicates that during the Second Indochina War, a man with no previous absence offenses tended to receive the same punishment treatment as a man with several previous offenses.

Military Justice and the Absence Offender:
the Clemency Board Sample

How do the results from the Notre Dame Survey compare with those of the Presidential Clemency board? The sample from the Presidential Clemency Board data is much larger and includes variables which are more suitable for quantitative analysis. Available dependent variables include the total months to which each man was sentenced and the total months for which he was confined as a result of absence offenses. Since some variables are similar to those in the Notre Dame Survey, it is possible to a certain extent to compare the two sets of results.

Results from the two separate data sets are to a considerable extent mutually confirming although the criteria for assessing degree of punishment are quite different. Just as the older portion of the Vietnam generation suffered more at the hands of their commanders for absences, so did they fare significantly less well when court-martialed. Though the Clemency Board data does not allow any comparison between men who were found guilty and those who were found innocent by a court-martial, it is possible to observe that among those who were found guilty of absence offenses by courts-martial, the ones who experienced this fate earlier in the war were more liable to receive and serve a longer sentence in a stockade or military prison (3-9).

There is no information in the PCB data about whether or not a man had attempted to avoid the draft prior to his induction, but there is evidence that men who had been conscripted did not fare as well as volunteers in the military courts. In the Notre Dame survey, there was a mild relationship between being a draftee and the severity of a commander's reaction to that man's absence offense. This relationship is reinforced by a relatively significant relationship between draftee status and a military court's sentencing of an absence offender. Military courts, as had commanders, showed a tendency to impose weaker sanctions on the G.I. with greater time in service (3-10).

While commanders were found to show judicial propriety in being more harsh in their dealings with offenders with longer absences in the Notre Dame data, they did not seem to take repetition of absences into account in their handling of offenders. That this may have been a ubiquitous condition among the managers of military justice is evidenced by a similar pattern of relationships among the variables in the Presidential Clemency Board data (3-10).

At this point, it should be noted that there exist for the variables considered differences in the degree of their correlation with months sentenced and months confined respectively. These differences between sentence and punishment reflect the flexibility of the system of military justice. The degree to which this flexibility exists for a particular group can be observed in the difference between the correlations with sentence and confinement for the variable which segregates the group. For instance, the weaker relationship of being a draftee to months confined as compared to the relation of being a draftee to months sentenced can be inferred to mean that those who had been drafted were a little less likely to serve their full sentence than other offenders (3-10). Overall, however, the general rigidity of the military justice system is illustrated in the Pearson's product moment correlation between months sentenced and months confined which is .863 and easily significant at the .001 level.

Besides reinforcing the findings of the Notre Dame Survey, analysis of the military justice variables from the Presidential Clemency Board reveals some additional attributes of the military justice system. For example, whites are somewhat more likely than nonwhites to have served their full sentences, but for the most part military courts were equally harsh when it came to sentencing both racial groups for their absence offenses. Additionally, the nature and location of a man's upbringing are shown to be of substantial importance to his fate at the hands of the military justice system. Southerners and men of rural origins are more likely to have received heavier sentences.

Just as the latter two conditions are generally associated with lower social class origins in American society, so are a number of other social variables found to be related to stiffer sentences and to the completion of such sentences. Family structural instability (which in the PCB sample includes such conditions as child abuse or parental alcoholism and illness), family economic instability, and having a greater number of siblings are variables which are related to harsher sentencing and which may thus indicate some class bias in the operation of military courts (3-8). Whether this bias in impact was the result of poorly organized defenses, a lack of social skills on the part of the lower class defendents, or aggravating circumstances in the commission of absence offenses cannot be determined by the analysis.

Among absence offenses, two branches of service—the Army and the Marine Corps—have previously been shown to be overly represented. In comparison to other branches of service, these two stand out as opposite extremes in the judicial processing of absence offenders.

Members of the Army who committed absence offenses were treated with comparative leniency in sentencing and were much more likely to serve shorter periods in confinement. With its emphasis on toughness and other manly virtues, the Marine Corps treated its absence offenders with comparative harshness. The Corps not only imposed more rigorous sentences on its absence offenders; it exhibited a tendency to exact the full weight of these sentences from its personnel. The fact that Marines are almost three times as numerous among deserters as they were among the armed forces as a whole during the Vietnam era suggests that harsher penalties may have been an attempt to keep a greater number of Marines from deserting—in which case it is probable that the harsher penalties had little to do with stemming the actual number of desertions (3-9).

Though evidence of gainful civilian employment during absence was not considered a mitigating factor in meting out punishment, voluntary surrender of the offender and not attempting to hide from authorities were apparently given due consideration in the limiting or extending of punishment. These instances of fairness are counterposed to the fact that men whom the Presidential Clemency Board certified as possessing legitimate physical and psychological problems involved in the motivation of their offense received and served more stringent sentences as a result of their courts-martial. Men who had previously been denied hardship discharges also served somewhat longer periods of imprisonment (3-10).

Summary

An attempt has been made to expand upon previous research on the Vietnam era deserter. An analysis of the data gathered in the Notre Dame survey showed that this material supports existent research on the men who illegally left their units during the Second Indochina War. By relating variables on the frequency and length of absence offenses from both the Notre Dame survey and the Presidential Clemency Board data to the social backgrounds and conditions of military service of the men in each sample, it was possible to delineate several patterns of desertion. This was followed by an inquiry into the workings of the military justice system that brought to light a number of social and institutional factors which may have affected the procedures by which the armed forces identified and punished absence offenders during the war.

Throughout these analyses, the theoretical themes adopted in Chapter One have proved useful in interpreting the empirical results. The same segments of the populace who posed a problem for the social integration of military units in World War II and Korea were a source of unit integration problems during the American involvement in Indochina. Just as those who began their lives in the lowest social strata found little success in civilian life, so did these same individuals disproportionately fail in the military. Indications are that certain individuals, hampered by class, race, and possibly region, were more likely to commit absence offenses.

Not only do these findings correspond to the theoretical perspective which defines individuals who have not undergone the "customary" socialization processes of American society, i.e. nuclear family and formal education, as more likely to fail to be integrated into military organizations; but it also supports the more radical contention that factors of social class were important in determining the distribution of suffering during the Second Indochina War.

Alienation and the breakdown of social control are shown to have been more influential to the desertion process than physical danger and personal hazard. Vietnam and combat veterans were more likely to go AWOL, not before or during the greatest threat to personal safety, but afterward. The psychological strain of military service itself, and not fear of the enemy, must be placed at the center of the desertion matrix. This particular point will become even clearer in the coming chapters when the relationship between Vietnam service and absent-without-leave offenses is further examined.

The purposive actor model with its emphasis on rational individuals possessing varying degrees of social competence receives an ironic form of support from the findings of these analyses. Social competence may not only be a factor in the level of achievement in institutionally sanctioned behavior; it may also determine the degree of success which an actor may experience in deviant behavior. Individuals with characteristics generally associated with greater social competence were less likely to pursue the unrewarding strategy of desertion, but when they did, they were more effective at it than their more socially deprived fellows.

It is possible that it may have been this social competency factor which resulted in men from the bottom of the social strata faring worse in the workings of the military justice system. Men who had already failed to master effective methods of behavior in other parts of the social system can be imagined to be particularly ill-suited to coping with the complicated machinations of military justice.

A Senate subcommittee's charge in 1969 that there was "a tendency on the part of some officials associated with the administration of military justice to place overemphasis on leniency"[19] may be justified by the results reported here. Particularly in the Army, deserters were receiving lower sentences, and this practice tended to increase as the war dragged on.

Another argument in support of the *internalized* nature of social control can be derived from the military justice outcomes for Marines. Although their longer sentences and greater likelihood of completing those sentences reveal a more repressive legal apparatus for dealing with absence offenses, the initial analysis in Chapter Two demonstrated that the rate of offense in the Marines was higher than in any other branch of service.

In terms of policy recommendations, no factor comes across with so much power at this point in the analysis as the variable of time. The Second Indochina War by American standards was long and costly. As the war dragged on, the patience of both the civilian and military populations was exhausted. In light of this fact, it is difficult to decide to which absence offender in terms of stage of the war when the offense was committed more tolerance is due. The man who went AWOL early in the war was likely to receive a harsher punishment for the same crime as that of his counterpart later in the war, while the offender later in the war was more likely to receive no hearing at all in a system overcrowded with offenders.

4

Dynamics of Desertion:
Vietnam Service and Absence Offenses

Among Vietnam-era deserters, there are two groups which have inspired respectively repulsion and sympathy from the general public. One group is made up of those who deserted from Vietnam assignments, either while in-country or while on leave. The reasons usually given for subjecting these men to special condemnation include the arguments that they abandoned their comrades and units in situations of real or potential peril and that some other young man had to be assigned to Vietnam to take each deserter's place. Only an estimated three percent of all Vietnam-era absence offenses were of this nature. Against the other group of deserters, neither the charge that they abandoned their comrades in peril nor the charge that others had to take their places can be made, because these men, who compose nearly twenty-three percent of all Vietnam-era absence offenders, served complete tours in Vietnam and only deserted after being returned to stateside assignments. Since the first group best fits the popular stereotype of deserters while the second group fits a less traditional image of desertion offenders, this chapter will attempt to show the real differences between the two groups by examining the complex relationship between service and desertion among the men who deserted after completing tours in the combat zone, and among others who deserted while still in the combat zone. A central question is: What could have caused so large a number of potential deserters to endure full tours in Indochina only to desert at a later time when they were assigned to presumably safer stateside posts?

Helmer, in his study of working class Vietnam veterans, argued that conditions of service in Vietnam were substantially different from conditions of service in previous wars.[1] Baskir and Strauss echo this assertion by picturing Indochina as a combat zone with built-in environmental deterrents to desertion.[2] These writers represent military service in Vietnam with its one-year rotation policies, long duration, and ideological cross-pressures as a social phenomenon unique in American history. This uniqueness may in the end constitute the only viable explanation for the patterns which relate Vietnam service to desertion during the Second Indochina War.

Using the Presidential Clemency Board data, which records both Vietnam service and location of last absence offense, results in a sample of 227 men suitable for this analysis.

The complexity of absence offense patterns in the context of service in Vietnam emerges in Table 4-1. Here it can be seen that a small group of men who went AWOL from Vietnam assignments and who were not discharged from active duty repeated their absence offense while in a stateside assignment. These men, along with the men who were discharged as a result of their absence offense while assigned to Vietnam, will be treated as one kind of offender. For analysis, these men will be labeled "in-country" offenders. Larger groups of men only committed absence offenses while assigned to stateside after completing one or more full tours in Indochina. In this analysis, these men will be labeled "stateside" offenders. Veterans in the first column in the fourth row who completed partial tours which were ended administratively will also be included in this "stateside" category. Here the central focus of this analysis will be to determine the extent to which men who committed absence offenses while assigned to a hazardous duty zone (the in-country deserters) can be sociologically distinguished from the men who deserted while assigned to stateside duty after completing an assignment in Indochina (the stateside deserters). Men who completed one or more tours in Indochina and committed an absence offense on a subsequent Indochina tour will be treated as a separate cate-

Table 4-1. **Record of Indochina Service and Location of Absence Offense (PCB)**

	Committed while Assigned to Stateside		Committed while Assigned to Indochina	
	N	(percent)	N	(percent)
One partial tour ending in AWOL	4	(1.8)	19	(8.4)
Finished one complete tour in Indochina	138	(60.8)	11	(4.8)
Finished more than one tour in Indochina	23	(10.1)	4	(1.8)
Completed partial tour in Vietnam (ended for administrative reasons)	22	(9.7)	6	(2.6)
Total	187	(82.4)	40	(17.6)

gory, "multiple-tour in-country" deserters. The breakdown of the sample into these three categories is shown in Table 4-2.

Social Background

Blacks were overrepresented among Vietnam-era deserters as a whole, and this overrepresentation also holds true for absence offenders with some amount of Indochina service. From this analysis, it seems that blacks were more likely to desert while assigned to Indochina on a first tour (4-3). The percentage of blacks who deserted while on a later tour in Vietnam falls between the percentage who deserted while on a first tour and the percentage who deserted while assigned to stateside subsequent to a Vietnam tour. The racial climate among U.S. troops in Indochina was a tense one with frequent eruptions of hostility. In the confrontations between blacks and whites, the armed forces itself was, because of the distribution of the two races among the ranks, perceived by many blacks as being a tool of the white establishment. As a black man progressed in rank and time on active duty, he became more and more an individual torn between militant young blacks in the lower ranks and his responsibilities as a soldier. A black man who had served at least one prior tour would therefore be expected to be less likely to desert while assigned to a combat zone for some reason associated with his being black than a black man on his first tour in the war that respected black leaders had already labeled "morally wrong."[3] Black men, therefore, particularly those on their first Vietnam tour, constitute one group who could be expected to be, and, in fact, were more likely to desert while assigned to Vietnam than to wait for return to a stateside base.

In a number of cases in other chapters, major social differences between groups of men were found to be related to early life experiences. Behavior in later life can often be traced to the structure of an individual's family. Even more relevant to later institutional behavior may be educational experiences. However, in comparing in-country and stateside deserters with

Table 4-2.	Categories of Desertion Used in Analysis (PCB)		
		N	(percent)
	In-country deserters	23	10.1
	Stateside deserters	183	80.6
	Multiple-tour	21	9.3
	Total	227	100.0

respect to two family-background variables and to years of education, no significant differences are revealed (4-4, 4-5). Multiple-tour in-country deserters are more likely to have come from homes where some type of instability was in evidence, but there is no clear theoretical explanation for this difference.

Military Personnel Histories

In addition to social-demographic differences between deserters and non-deserters, other chapters have indicated that absence offenders were more likely to have certain types of personnel histories. This analysis, in contrasting the combat zone deserter with his post-Vietnam counterpart, considers four personnel history variables — intake into services, age at induction, time in service, record of hardship reassignment requests, and type of Vietnam assignment.

While a "conflict view" of military desertion might predict higher rates of absence offenses among conscripts, the Presidential Clemency Board report estimated that approximately eighty percent of Vietnam-era deserters had volunteered for military service (4-6). In the present context, the conflict possibility is still worth considering. Its logic is as follows. Volunteers who found themselves pushed to desert by the pressures of Vietnam service would be more likely than a draftee to resist such tendencies. The volunteer in this case might be more likely to view his enlistment as a mistake which he consciously made. In this same situation, the draftee might feel himself to be more a victim of institutional mechanisms and less bound by a personal commitment of responsibility than the volunteer. Based on the Presidential Clemency Board data, draftees were indeed significantly more likely to desert while on a first tour to Vietnam.

Previous studies have suggested that because of their immaturity younger men are frequently less well integrated into their military units than their older counterparts.[4] Desertion from an Indochina assignment is, however, associated with somewhat older soldiers who were inducted. This can, of course, be explained by the fact that men were not normally drafted until after they turned nineteen.

To a certain extent, time in service is a variable whose distribution is determined by procedural constraints related to the dependent variable. Until 1972, a completed tour in Indochina constituted twelve months of military service by itself. An individual would not be assigned to Vietnam until after he had completed basic training and advanced individual training. An examination of the mean months in service for each of the three categories of absence offenders reveals that the difference between the time in service for stateside deserters and the other two categories is very significant (4-7). Stateside deserters are revealed to be a true historical irony in that their average time in service is almost identical to the service required of Army enlistees and considerably more than the two years required of draftees.

Another factor which might have an effect on whether a man deserted under the pressures of Vietnam or deferred such behavior until after completion of his tour of duty is his relationship to the military personnel system. A variable which could reflect this aspect of a soldier's personnel history is his record of hardship reassignment requests. A breakdown on this variable for each category of deserter shows no differences significant at the .05 level, with none of the groups of deserters demonstrating a tendency to utilize existing bureaucratic channels for coping with conflicts between personal and system needs (4-8).

The commonsense assumption that greater deprivation can be associated with lower morale has been repeatedly refuted by research.[5] In this sample, men who deserted while assigned to Indochina were twice as likely to be serving in noncombat rather than in combat roles while in Vietnam. This information either confirms previous research on morale and deprivation or is indicative of the increased difficulty of desertion while engaged with the enemy in the Indochinese setting. The large number of missing cases for this variable is a function of the blurring of combat and noncombat designations in Vietnam, a distinction made even more difficult when coding from personnel files (4-9).

Motivations for Absence Offenses

Each individual appearing before the Presidential Clemency Board was allowed to state his reasons for committing his offense. For the absence offenders considered in this analysis, all but ten offered one of twenty-four reasons for their offenses. The breakdown by stated reason for offense and the subsequent classification of these reasons are shown in Table 4-10. General reason for offense by type of offender is displayed in Table 4-11. Although it may be apparent to some readers that the categories are to a degree overlapping or ambiguous, it should be stressed that this research is totally restricted to the perceptions and labels of the members of the Presidential Clemency Board.

Table 4-10.   **Stated Reason for Offense (PCB)**

	N	(percent)
Ideological motivation		
Opposition to war in general	2	(0.9)
Opposition to war in Vietnam	4	(1.8)
Military-related motivation		
Dislike of military service	11	(4.8)
Hindrance or denial of reassignment requests	10	(4.4)
Unable to meet intellectual demands of job*	2	(0.9)
Deception in recruitment process	7	(3.1)
Denied leave	2	(0.9)
Subject to procedural unfairness	13	(5.7)
Denied reassignment to Vietnam	1	(0.4)
Personal problems as motivation		
Post-combat psychological problems	16	(7.0)
Drug dependency (including alcoholism)	16	(7.0)
Medical problems	4	(1.8)
Emotional problems	16	(7.0)
Family problems (marital)	17	(7.5)
Family medical problems	21	(9.3)
Family psychological problems	7	(3.1)
Family financial problems	15	(6.6)
Other family problems	20	(8.8)
Motivations of a selfish nature		
Did not want to return to Indochina	2	(0.9)
Did not like Vietnam	5	(2.2)
Avoidance of punishment	1	(0.4)
Boredom	6	(2.6)
No stated reason	28	(12.3)

*Both men were inducted under Project 100,000 which allowed men with I.Q.'s below minimum standards to serve.

Table 4-11.   **Type of Stated Motivation and Type of Offender (PCB)**

	Type of Offender		
Type of Motivation	In-Country	Stateside	Multiple-Tour In-Country
Ideological	3 (13.0 percent)	2 (1.1 percent)	1 (4.8 percent)
Military-related	3 (13.0 percent)	38 (20.8 percent)	5 (23.8 percent)
Personal	4 (17.4 percent)	41 (22.4 percent)	7 (33.3 percent)
Family	8 (34.7 percent)	68 (37.2 percent)	4 (19.0 percent)
Selfish	3 (13.0 percent)	10 (5.5 percent)	3 (14.3 percent)
No stated reason	2 (8.7 percent)	24 (13.2 percent)	1 (4.8 percent)
Total	23	183	21

Major differences in stated motivations for offense are few. Most apparent are the small percentages of stateside offenders who were ideologically or selfishly motivated. Multiple-tour in-country deserters were somewhat more likely to state personal problems or problems with the military as motivation for their offenses.

Conclusions

The central question considered in this chapter was whether differences existed between men who deserted while assigned to Indochina and men who completed their Indochina tours only to desert from stateside assignments. If major differences *had* been in evidence, it would have supported the suggestion of Edward Shils that the Vietnam-era deserter is no different from deserters of previous wars.[6] As previously noted, Shils argued that Vietnam-era desertion, as desertion in previous wars, was the result of certain soldiers being poorly integrated into all the institutions in their social environment. Under this theoretical perspective, it would seem logical that men who finished their tours before deserting should have been more socially well-integrated than those who deserted while assigned to Vietnam.

Partial evidence for the validity of the social integration perspective can be found in the results given here. Nonwhite Americans were significantly more likely to desert while serving their first tour in Vietnam, though there was little difference between the two groups with respect to other social background variables. The role of integration into the military itself was shown to be important by the relationship between time in service and not deserting while assigned to Indochina. This is reasonable since men who had more time in service before going to Southeast Asia were more likely to have internalized norms and values of the service. Men who did not desert while assigned to Vietnam may have also been those more likely to utilize conventional personnel channels such as applying for hardship reassignment, even though such applications were rare in all categories.

Less supportive of the idea that Vietnam deserters were no more than social misfits is the association of both ideological motivation and being drafted with in-country desertion. A personnel specialist might cautiously advise the military to use only ideologically-committed volunteers in any future international police actions. Assigning personnel to non-combat zone assignments for a period of time prior to overseas assignments might also prove a method of reducing combat zone desertions.

The degree to which these three categories of deserters are similar re-

inforces the idea that Indochina was an environment with built-in deterrents to desertion. Deserting in a land with an alien culture and generally
hostile populace is certainly not comparable to an American deserting in
a European theater.

Finally, the material treated in this chapter must serve as a reminder of
the complexity of service and desertion during the Second Indochina War.
The existence of stateside and multiple-tour in-country deserters is a fact
of which few Americans are aware.

5

Dynamics of Desertion: Four Special Types of Offenders

This chapter will deal with four special types of offenders. Its purpose will be to further develop a sociological understanding of the men who have become living symbols and targets of America's disdain for the progress and outcome of the Second Indochina War. Too often these men have been viewed with a false commonality. Here four of the most distinct subgroups of Vietnam offenders will be isolated as examples of the considerable diversity of the men who were the subject of the amnesty debate. Jehovah's Witnesses, Vietnam veterans, mental rejects, and men labeled as criminals have been selected to demonstrate that the amnesty issue is not one that can be regarded with moralistic simplicity.

The Religious Offenders

Perhaps no other religious group in the history of the United States has more consistently defied the powers of government than have the Jehovah's Witnesses. President Truman's amnesty board refused to accept the Witnesses' religious objection to World War II because they had refused "to yield (their) opinion to that of organized society."[1] The period of the Vietnam War, marked by its heavy reliance on the Selective Service system for the provision of manpower, proved no exception in the struggle between this group, with its consistent resistance to secular authority, and the federal government. Confrontation was inevitable. As one student of the sect stated, "the Jehovah's Witnesses reject as hopelessly evil all governments now in existence, as well as any others that human efforts may create."[2] Under the leadership of General Hershey, the Selective Service system was willing to tolerate no institutional impediment to its task of filling the ranks for a very unpopular war.[3] Of the two major religious institutions to refuse induction (the other was the Black Muslim faith), the Witnesses were the more numerous and figure prominently among those individuals processed by the Ford Clemency Board.

Researchers have found it difficult to obtain data on the members of the sect.[4] The files on the Jehovah's Witnesses who applied to the clemency board reveal a greater percentage of missing details than those of other applicants. It is not unlikely that the church, in giving its consent to its members to participate in the clemency program, may have also stipulated that information given to the board be kept to a minimum.

Of the Presidential Clemency Board sample of 468 civilian offenders, ninety-three or about twenty percent listed their religious preference as Jehovah's Witness. Previous work has suggested that Jehovah's Witnesses are somewhat below the national average in education and income (5-1, 5-2). Though there are few college graduates and students in the sample, it should be noted that the percentage of high school graduates is not very different from the national statistic.[5] Information on occupation is more obviously absent than that on education, but the predominance of blue collar workers is evident among the cases for which there is data.

Just as important as a sociological description of the Jehovah's Witnesses among the draft offenders are measures of their similarity to other offenders. As a group the Jehovah's Witnesses tend to be less educated than other draft offenders. Though Jehovah's Witnesses are unlikely to be employed in white collar occupations, they are no more likely to have blue collar occupations than other draft offenders (5-8). This finding underscores the similarity of all draft offenders to the general population.

In general, draft offenders are not prone to the social background problems characteristic of military offenders, and the Jehovah's Witnesses are no exception (5-3). The Jehovah's Witnesses in the sample provided little evidence of the several kinds of problems which would have gained them more lenient treatment by the Clemency Board. The existence of family background problems is no different for Jehovah's Witnesses than for other draft offenders. When it comes to more immediate personal problems of a physical, psychological, or economic nature which might have been related to the evasion offense, there is a significant absence of evidence of such problems among Jehovah's Witnesses (5-3, 5-8). This is not surprising, since it has already been assumed that religion was the major motivating factor in the Witnesses' draft resistance.

The Jehovah's Witnesses were more likely to be married than other offenders (5-4). Racially, the Jehovah's Witnesses in the sample approach the national demographic pattern, and their ages are approximately the same as other draft offenders (5-5). The largest percentage of all civilian offenders, twenty-five percent, spent their childhood in the Ninth Circuit court district.[6] This also held true for the Jehovah's Witnesses in the sample with twenty-one percent coming from the Pacific Coast states.

For the most part, Jehovah's Witnesses supplied few details to the Presidential Clemency Board concerning their arrest and trial. Still, from the limited data available, a clear pattern emerges. The Jehovah's Witnesses in the sample tended to turn themselves in rather than await apprehension (5-6). Only one reported that he had gone into hiding, and he, it should be added, did not attempt to leave the country. Finally a majority of those for whom information is available pled either guilty or nolo contendre when they appeared in court.

As for the disposition of the Jehovah's Witnesses as defendents, while most were sentenced to a period of imprisonment ranging from a few months to five years, a smaller proportion were actually incarcerated. A good portion of these, however, spent over a year in prison. Probation was apparently a much more common punishment, with all but eighteen of the Jehovah's Witnesses in the sample serving at least some period of time on probation and a majority serving over two years (5-7).

In comparison to other types of draft offenders, it is evident that, in general, Jehovah's Witnesses, who for religious reasons did not register with the Selective Service System or refused induction, fared no worse with respect to sentencing, imprisonment, and time on probation than did others. At the same time, those Jehovah's Witnesses in this sample met no special moderation or leniency in their dealings with the American judicial process (5-7), (5-8).

Baskir and Strauss and President Carter[7] in his pardon of draft offenders acknowledged the existence of a large number of nonregistrants who had successfully managed to evade official detection. Assuming that the majority of Jehovah's Witnesses demonstrated their absence of allegiance for the United States government by passively ignoring the selective service office at their eighteenth birthday, the large number of Jehovah's Witnesses among those convicted of draft evasion charges may indicate a systematic searching out of this religious group by local boards. Even if this is the case, the institutionalized processing of these men as federal criminals constitutes a milder form of punishment than the mob actions so frequently directed against this group during previous wars.

While President Ford's clemency program and President Carter's 1977 pardon effectively relieved the plight of the Jehovah's Witnesses who resisted conscription during the Vietnam War, the fact remains that a group of men consisting mostly of blue collar workers and heads of households were systematically punished by the institutions of government for clinging to the tenets of an established religion. Beyond any discussion of the compatibility of such anti-state religions and the modern state remains the evidence of a massive bureaucracy's potential to execute government policy in an impartial, dispassionate, and efficient manner.

The War Veterans

Chapter Four compared military offenders who had deserted when assigned to Vietnam with those servicemen who completed Vietnam tours and deserted after return to stateside assignments. The major questions asked in that chapter were what factors precipitated desertion on one hand and delayed it on the other. In the present context, attention will return to that significant proportion of absence offenders who had completed Vietnam service and currently retain less-than-honorable discharges as a result of their violations. Through a more intense analysis of the information on this group of military offenders, it should be possible to delineate the degree to which these men as a group are typical of military absence offenders or may merit special consideration in any future amnesty-related policy actions.

The Vietnam service histories of the military offenders in the Presidential Clemency Board sample are summarized in Table 5-9. In all, 26.6 percent of the men spent at least some period of active duty service in Vietnam. One hundred ninety-five or nineteen percent of the men completed at least one full tour in Vietnam. Seventy-three or 7.2 percent served partial tours. Some of these men's tours ended in absence offenses, but a larger portion had tours which ended for reasons other than absence or injury. Included in this group were some men with drug problems who participated in military rehabilitation programs and men who received administrative transfers based on health and family difficulties, but most such administrative transfers during the Vietnam War resulted from shifting government policies with respect to American troop commitment. In the later years of the war, units were regularly removed from Vietnam and frequently the men in these units experienced an appropriate reduction of tour. Still for the purposes of this analysis, only those individuals who completed full tours and those whose tours ended in injury will be regarded as having fulfilled Vietnam service.

Those who fulfilled Vietnam service differ significantly on a number of variables from other absence offenders. Readily discerned and easily explained are a number of chronological factors. In the previous chapter, it was revealed that men who deserted after serving in Vietnam understandably had spent more time on active duty than those who deserted in Vietnam. This longer period on active duty likewise distinguishes them from all absence offenders in general. Again, this is a function of two things. First, the tour in Vietnam itself typically accounts for twelve months of service, and second, it was suggested that there might exist a greater commitment to the military institution among these Vietnam veterans. This longer time on active duty may to some extent account for the facts that these men tended to come from the older portion of the Vietnam generation, that their offenses were more apt to occur later in the war, and that they were more likely to have left active duty at a later date than did other military offenders. The importance of these chronological factors is underscored by the fact that these men were inducted into service at a younger age than other offenders (5-10).

Since these men enlisted at a younger age than most offenders and were older than other offenders at the time of application for clemency, they must have served earlier in the Vietnam War. The typical Vietnam veteran deserter enlisted as a young man early in the war. He left the United States in the flurry of patriotism that dominated the public spirit at the outbreak of the war. His return to stateside brought him into contact with a declining public enthusiasm for the war. His youth, the trauma of Vietnam, and his commitment to the military organization would have provided the contradictory forces which set the stage for his subsequent desertion.

In terms of social background, the Vietnam veteran offender differs only slightly from other military offenders. Vietnam veteran offenders are racially comparable to absence offenders in general, meaning that blacks are more prevalent among them than in the population as a whole. They are somewhat better educated than other offenders and more likely to be from the northern and western sections of the nation. Intellectually, in terms of IQ and Armed Forces Qualifying Test (AFQT) categories, they rank higher than other offenders. This is very important since it means that Vietnam veteran absence offenders are not likely to be members of Project 100,000.[8] Those who speak of Vietnam veteran offenders and Project 100,000 offenders as two separate categories of absence offenders are therefore quite correct in doing so.[9] While their childhoods were significantly less liable to be marked by family instability or economic deprivation, they are much more likely to report personal problems of a physical or psychological nature related to their offense (5-11).[10]

A closer examination of these physical and psychological problems shows that for a majority among those who reported having problems these problems were psychological in nature. Though drug and alcohol problems were reported, neither type of problem appears to have been so important as the psychological reaction to Vietnam and military service. When the Presidential Clemency Board asked about all psychological problems, not just those related to absence offenses, sixty-nine of the Vietnam veterans in the sample produced evidence of such problems. Fifty-eight percent of these psychological problems could be definitely or possibly attributed to a Vietnam origin. Another twenty percent could be linked to military service. In twenty-nine or fifty-two percent of the forty-six cases reporting non-psychological medical difficulties, such troubles could be traced to the man's Vietnam service. The staff of the Presidential Clemency Board after examining these men's cases felt obligated to state that almost all these men suffered from some aspect of the psychological condition then known as Post-Vietnam Syndrome (5-12). [11]

For the Presidential Clemency Board sample of military offenders, a significantly negative relationship exists between being a Vietnam veteran and being drafted indicating that the Vietnam veterans in the sample were significantly more likely to have volunteered for Vietnam service than other types of offenders. A breakdown of Vietnam veteran offenders with respect to the channel by which they entered active duty shows that most had enlisted for three years and a considerable number had reenlisted (5-13). Their initial commitment to military service was thus through a voluntary contract, but sometime during the fulfillment of this contract, following service in Vietnam, these men attempted to abrogate their commitment through flight. There exists no significant correlation between being a post-Vietnam deserter and having applied for either conscientious objector status or a hardship discharge. Evidence in Chapter Seven will show that attempts to use the personnel structure to one's advantage after induction were consistently ineffective. Hence, these men's disenchantment with legitimate channels of escape from active duty may have empirical justification.

In Chapter Three, it was noted that veterans of Vietnam were, in comparison to other offenders, likely to report a greater number of absence without leave offenses, yet they reported no significantly larger number of total months AWOL. In other words, Vietnam returnees were more prone to go AWOL but less apt to stay AWOL. Despite their tendency to repeat their offenses, there is some indication that the system did exhibit some degree of leniency toward these men. In Chapter Three, it was reported that in the end, the military did not show special mercy to Vietnam veterans; however, the picture is more complex than this as a more detailed analysis reveals. Compared to all other offenders, Vietnam returnees are significantly more likely to have gone AWOL at some time and experienced no punishment. They also evidence a significantly greater number of non-judicial or Article Fifteen punishments for AWOL, and, in addition, Vietnam veterans were less likely than other offenders to receive a general court-martial. In other words, the initial absence offenses of Vietnam returnees may have been overlooked by their stateside commanders. Even repetition of the offense met with the lowest level of punishment available under the Uniform Code of Military Justice (5-14). Such lenience, however, could have done little to alleviate the conditions which initially motivated the Vietnam veteran to go AWOL. In the end, large numbers of Vietnam veterans did receive a court martial and, inevitably, the less-than-honorable discharge which nullified the political service that they had rendered their nation.

At least, the final judgment spared the majority of the Vietnam veteran offenders incarceration in military prisons. Sixty-nine percent of these men received no sentence other than their less-than-honorable discharge, and somewhat fewer of them were not even incarcerated while awaiting trial (5-15). Though none of the Vietnam returnees served more than a year in military prison, it must be remembered that the stigma of a bad discharge and the loss of veterans benefits, especially for those with physical and psychological problems, constitute severe sentences which are in fact "life" sentences.

Personnel from Project 100,000

Prior to the Vietnam War, the United States military had screened from service men whose Armed Forces Qualifying Test (AFQT) scores and other measures of intelligence indicated a level of social competence not sufficient for an efficient performance of military duties. The operation of Project 100,000 described in Chapter Two provided an exception to this tradition, and this section will more closely examine the large proportion of absence offenders who entered active duty under the auspices of this program. In following the practice of the Presidential Clemency Board, this report must emphasize that this is not an analysis of all 240,000 of those individuals who entered military service through Project 100,000 nor can it be accepted as an indicator of the project's overall success or failure. The project was, however, officially discontinued in 1972, and its inductees are overly represented among the absence offenders in the clemency board sample. [12]

The program allowed most individuals from AFQT Category IV to be inducted, but a very small percentage (1.7) of Project 100,000 absence offenders were classified as Category V, the lowest category. The presence of several individuals with intelligence quotients of 50 or below in the sample should be regarded as tragic exceptions rather than as typical cases. For the majority of these men, the Department of Defence's attempt to ameliorate their life chances should not offhandedly be regarded as insincere.

A number of social background characteristics distinguished these men from other absence offenders. From the racial breakdown of Project 100,000 personnel in Table 5-16, the exceptionally large number of blacks in this group (over three times their representation in the American population as a whole) can be seen.

Region of origin as well as ethnic background sets these offenders apart from others. A significant positive relationship between being from the South and Project 100,000 status was obtained by classifying only those clemency board applicants who grew up in the fourth and fifth circuit court districts as southern. This fails to include such states as Kentucky, Tennessee, Arkansas, and Missouri as southern, but still demonstrates that the lower IQs of all southerners and minority members from other regions made them more highly represented in Project 100,000 (5-17).

Men in Project 100,000 are less likely to have grown up in homes where both natural parents were present, but they are also somewhat less likely than other offenders to have grown up in homes where there was evidence of other types of instability. They are a little more likely, however, to have come from backgrounds with evidence of economic deprivation. Not unexpectedly, these men constitute the most poorly educated group in a sample marked by generally low educational levels. This is evidenced by a significant negative correlation between years of education and Project 100,000 membership (5-17).

Where the group of Vietnam veterans examined in the previous section showed a propensity to have volunteered for military service, the members of Project 100,000 were more likely to have been drafted than other absence offenders. Still, the rule that most absence offenders joined the military voluntarily also holds for this group of men (5-18). It is, however, ironic that a group of men so unsuitable for military service should have been more likely to have been legally coerced onto active duty. Perhaps it is the higher percentage of draftees among the Project 100,000 personnel which accounts for their being older at entrance to active duty than other absence offenders who, on the whole, tended to enlist at an early age. The fact that Project 100,000 did not get started until 1967 could have also created an additional two-year delay in the eligibility of Project participants. Project 100,000 personnel were more likely to have served in the Army even if they enlisted. This is to be expected, as the Army has traditionally been noted for its lower intellectual requirements for enlistment in comparison to the more technically oriented Navy and Air Force, but the extremely low representation of Marines among the Project 100,000 personnel in the sample is more surprising, especially given the overrepresentation of Marines in the sample as a whole noted in Chapter Two. The significant negative relation between Project 100,000 membership and time in service stands as one more comment on the failure of the project. Even compared with other absence offenders, the short duration of the service which these men were able to render the nation is distinct (5-19).

Another interesting difference between the Project 100,000 personnel and the Vietnam veterans in the sample can be seen in the nature of their absence offenses. Vietnam veterans went AWOL a greater number of times than other offenders yet showed no greater number of total months AWOL. Project 100,000 personnel went AWOL fewer times than other offenders, but spent a greater number of months absent without leave. A few individual cases which describe Project 100,000 personnel as being unable to complete basic training or in one instance taking up to nine months to complete the normally eight-week course,[13] may provide the basis for an explanation: since neither group showed a greater inclination to go into hiding or surrender voluntarily (5-19), it may be assumed that military authorities, or local commanders, may not have considered the Project 100,000 personnel as "worth" picking up. In fact, among military professionals, there was widespread discontent about the program from its outset.[14] Chances are that men who were mentally unable to meet Army basic training standards did not present much possibility of becoming useful members of the armed forces through the workings of the military justice system. From this data, it may be assumed that once these soldiers were returned to military control, they were as expeditiously as possible given their less-than-honorable discharges and returned to the civilian world, without having been turned into the more useful citizens described in the lofty goals of Project 100,000. Overall though, these men received no more or less stringent punishment than other absence offenders at the hands of military courts (5-18).

The Common Criminals

While the three other groups of men treated in this chapter have some potential for a certain amount of public sympathy, the final group is the one most often spotlighted by opponents of any kind of amnesty. These are the men for whom an absence offense constituted only an additional crime in a deviant career. Tables 5-20 and 5-21 show the breakdowns of absence offenders with respect to non-absence offenses. Of the military absence offenders in the sample, 116 or 11.5 percent of them have civilian criminal records. Almost forty-five percent of these 116 have convictions for violent felonies.

The percentage of the sample of military absence offenders who have a record of non-absence military offenses is substantially larger than the percentage who have a record of civilian crime. Many (29.9 percent) of these offenders were handled by nonjudicial punishment or Article 15's indicating only the most minor infractions, while only eight men received a general court-martial indicating the most severe of offenses. Another factor which may be considered important in examining military offenses is the twofold nature of the military justice system. The Uniform Code of Military Justice covers two kinds of crimes—those which have an equivalent in the civilian world and those which are particularly military in nature. As can be seen in Table 5-22, a very small number of the absence offenders committed acts which would have been crimes outside the context of the military establishment. Sixty-eight percent of all non-absence military offenses were committed prior to the man's first absence offense, indicating that a number of these men may have been motivated to go AWOL by other difficulties that they were having with the structure of military authority. It should also be noted that the correlation between having been convicted of a civilian crime and having been convicted of a non-absence military offense is not significant (5-23).

One question that might be asked concerning the men with civilian criminal records and other military offenses is the degree to which they fall into the two previously discussed categories of Vietnam veterans and Project 100,000 personnel. Vietnam veterans and Project 100,000 inductees in the sample are no more or no less likely than other offenders to have been convicted of a civilian crime or a non-absence military offense (5-24). Hence advocates of special consideration for the first two groups of absence offenders can conveniently sidestep the "common criminal" charges of their opponents.

But what of these absence offenders who have either a civilian criminal record or who have been convicted of other types of military offenses? How they differ from or are similar to other absence offenders is revealing.

Though the relationships are generally weak, there are discernable differences between men who committed civilian and military crimes and other offenders. While those who have non-absence military offenses differ from other offenders only by being older, those with civilian criminal records differ slightly from other offenders by being somewhat younger and by having fewer years of education. They are more likely to be nonwhite. The combined effect of a less-than-honorable discharge and a criminal record is evidenced by their greater likelihood of lacking fulltime employment at the time that they applied to the Presidential Clemency Board (5-23).

An examination of conditions of service reveals more differences. Both groups of men tend to have enlisted at a younger age than other absence offenders. Those who have civilian criminal records are somewhat less likely than other absence offenders to have applied for a hardship discharge while on active duty, and their total months of absence from active duty without leave tend to be less than others. Otherwise, in conditions of service and in their absence offenses, they are very similar to absence offenders in general (5-25).

Those personnel with non-absence military offenses differ from other absence offenders in a number of ways. First, they have more months of creditable service than other absence offenders. They are more likely to be veterans of the Marine Corps. These men are rare among absence offenders in being somewhat more likely to have applied for hardship discharges from active service (5-25). Perhaps, it is their record of conflict with the military system which accounts for their marked tendency to go AWOL repeatedly and their hesitation to return to military control voluntarily.

Two groups of men have been examined in this section. One smaller group had been found guilty of crimes against society as a whole, but a much larger group have been found guilty of crimes against one institution within the society, the military establishment. No doubt, both of these groups will be the subject of specific considerations in the continuing debates over post-Vietnam amnesty programs.

Summary

This chapter has selectively dealt with four groups of offenders. The purpose of treating such very diverse groups is foremost to emphasize the social differences which divide the men processed and negatively labeled by national institutions during the Second Indochina War.

The experiences of the Jehovah's Witnesses are noteworthy because they clearly demonstrate how a group of men belonging to a religious organization have been caught in a clash between their church and the political institutions which that church refuses to recognize. Their processing and punishment — and even their repatriation — is a collective phenomenon. The actors involved are not individuals but institutions — two corporate actors, one commanding greater loyalty, the other greater force.

Another group of men provided the greatest service that the military institution could ask of them. Its members served a tour of duty in a war-torn country with an alien climate and culture. As a result of providing that service, they were no longer able to provide what is considered less rigorous stateside service. Collectively they share the same malady. Distinctive traits on a number of criteria mark them off from other men. Collectively they share the same fate.

Measured intelligence is a tricky sort of phenomenon. Its uneven distribution in the population is almost perfectly defined by measurable social factors. Many gateways to social mobility are guarded by its real-world manifestations of "number-two lead" pencils and computerized forms. However, when military personnel needs threatened deferments for middle-class students, liberal politicians were willing to expose men who had not adapted in civilian life to the much more demanding social world of military service. It is ironic that this liberal program of the "Great Society" left many of its alumni worse off in terms of life chances than they had been before.

A number of additional points can also be made. The case of the Jehovah's Witnesses was included as an example of how easily the legal system could arrest, try, and imprison almost the whole male generation of a religious body. Accomplished quietly with little or no public outcry, this methodical judicial treatment of a dissident sect still lies beyond the knowledge of most Americans. Perhaps, it as so many other events was made invisible by the kaleidoscope of social change which surrounded the war.

The analysis of the Vietnam veterans and the Project 100,000 members has shown the degree to which these two groups differ. Both compose large percentages of the men with less-than-honorable discharges from the Vietnam era, and both are decidedly different from the stereotypic view of Vietnam deserters. The unique situations of each of these groups make them particularly subject to public compassion; together they make up over half of this sample of military absence offenders.

Finally, the so-called "common criminal" element of the absence offender population was examined. Those of its members who have been found guilty of crimes which have equivalents in civil society are surprisingly few, especially when it is considered that twenty-eight percent of the men in Illinois state prisons are veterans.[15] A larger percentage was found guilty of crimes which are particularly military in nature. These are crimes, such as their common crime of going absent-without-leave, which they could not have committed in civilian society.

At the close of this, the last of three chapters on the Vietnam offender, it is appropriate to sum up findings and place these findings in the context of the theoretical perspectives which were adopted in Chapter One.

From the functional perspective, the personnel problem of the Second Indochina War was to induct men who could be merged into the organizational structures necessary for the conduct of military operations. According to the work of Shils and Janowitz, the organizational charts which depict fire teams, squads, platoons, companies, and batallions only cease to be the imaginary fantasies of executive officers when these institutional formats are given social reality by an underlying system of primary relationships.[16] In other words, bureaucratic action is given substance not by duty rosters, but by the emotions and commitments of feeling, flesh and blood beings. From previous research, it is evident that certain social attributes make humans more amenable to integration into artificial social units.

In the military context, desertion is the extreme indication that such integration has failed. Not surprisingly, the results from this research just as the results of previous research have shown that the major predictors of integration into military units during the Second Indochina War are the same predictors of integration into other modern complex organizations. Members of minorities, men from the disintegrated families of the lower classes, men from the cultural periphery (such as the South), men with fewer years of education, and those who failed to score highly on standard measures of intelligence were all more likely to have demonstrated their resistance to being integrated into military units by deserting.

One factor important to social integration is consistent, stable contact. Throughout this analysis time and stability have proven crucial ingredients in the socialization of the American soldier. Time in service prior to a tour in Vietnam could have helped prevent desertions in two ways. Soldiers who spent time in the day-to-day routine of a stateside or European assignment had time to become accustomed to the peculiar aspects of military life. After the initial rigors of training and without the pressure of being assigned to Indochina, such men could come to think of themselves as soldiers through an almost-leisurely process of socialization. Second, time in service prior to Indochina, at least for a one term enlistee or conscript, translates into less time in service after Vietnam. The large number of men who deserted from stateside assignments after serving in Indochina testifies to the wisdom of a personnel program adopted late in the war which deducted weeks or up to several months from the military obligations of men returning from Vietnam tours.

Another set of findings can best be interpreted from a conflict perspective. Again time was revealed to be a consequential element in the analysis. For an undeclared war with unclear objectives, the Second Indochina War lasted too long. What at the beginning of the war were manageable sources of conflict became with the passage of time serious conditions of disintegration in military organization. Desertions increased dramatically. An overloaded military justice system became increasingly ineffective and capricious. With American society undergoing an economic boom and popular culture reflecting a growing hedonism, the military apparatus with its dependency on citizen soldiers began to crack at the level of the individual.

A policy manifestation of this trend was the eventual decision to withdraw conscripts from the Indochina theater. From the functional perspective, however, it is less clear what the policy toward conscripts should have been. For against the fact of conscript dissatisfaction with service in Vietnam must be weighed the military's own requirements at the time for large numbers of soldiers—soldiers who probably would not have been available without the draft.

In order to fill personnel needs, men who had already been labeled mentally unsuitable for participation in the mainstream of American life were lured or drafted into the armed forces through Project 100,000. The effect on morale of placing these men who fit Roger Little's "dud" description side by side with other soldiers was nothing less than devastating.

That military service was an alienating experience in the material sense of the term alienation, rather than any ideological sense, is indicated by the stated motivations and real life conditions of absence offenders. Going AWOL was not so often a verbalized political activity as it was a manifestation of the opposition between personal interests and the interests of the state. Servicemen sometimes qualified for welfare benefits as military pay rates lagged behind the economic vitality of the civilian sector. As has been seen in their social backgrounds as well as their stated reasons for their actions, deserters at some point gave in to personal needs. Only commitments to organizational goals and interpersonal loyalties to fellow soldiers made the difference between a deserter and an honorably discharged veteran. The social class aspect of American military disintegration during the Second Indochina War has repeatedly received support from the results of the analyses in the forgoing chapters. In World War II, the entire population shared the costs of the war. In the Korean War, the military participation ratio was much lower, and the personnel for the war were taken from a socially lower segment of the population. Korea was like World War II without the top of the service distribution. In the Second Indochina War, the ratio of service was even lower, and the induction mechanism dug even deeper into the lower strata of the American class structure.

Veterans from the Second Indochina War with less-than-honorable discharges for absence offenses represent the degree to which the Selective Service System and the recruitment programs dug too low. As Baskir and Strauss note, many of these men wouldn't have made it at their first jobs in civilian life.[17] However, no other first job could leave a man with the lifetime stigma associated with a less-than-honorable discharge.

Black Americans, who shared least in the benefits brought by the existence of the American political structure, paid most heavily its costs. As a result of their lower socioeconomic status, they were more likely to serve and more likely to die (5-26). They were also more likely to get a less-than-honorable discharge.

Formal mechanisms of social control grew more and more erratic in their operation at the time when internal mechanisms of control were most weakened. In fact, it is doubtful that the punishment of those who took flight served as any deterrence to others. First, a large portion of those who took flight were Vietnam veterans, men who would not have been especially cowed by the threat of military justice. As for that other sizable part of the absence offender population, the men whose intellectual skills sometimes led them to have difficulty with basic training, the potential complications of bad discharges must have seemed as foreign as the cause for which they served. The futility of harsher responses to the growing discord is well illustrated by the failure of the Marine Corps to stem desertion despite an uncomparable stringency in its treatment of offenders.

Second, as could be seen by the incarceration statistics for the Vietnam veterans, the real imprisonment factor was less than it could have been. Despite the fact that military punishment, as judged by the conditions at Presidio alone, could be horrendous and inhumane, it could have been worse. That career military men must have frequently shown compassion in their roles as military adjudicators is evidenced by the large number of undesirable discharges with minimum confinement and the extreme dissatisfaction of a punishment-thirsty Congress.

In a special subcommittee report from the U.S. Senate Committee on the Armed Services in 1969, senators stated that, after analyzing the treatment of deserters, they were "of the opinion there is a lack of appreciation on the part of some in the Department of Defense as to the seriousness of the problem." This group of senators put themselves on record as strongly

opposing what they felt was "a tendency on the part of some officials associated with the administration of military justice to place overemphasis
on leniency."[18]

Despite the conclusions of this Senate subcommittee and other defense
"hard-liners," the analyses conducted in chapters Two through Five reveal
several distinct groups of absence offenders with social profiles more so-
licitous of compassion. Going to war can be the greatest test of human
social character, and the men least likely to cope with this test were frequently those members of the Vietnam generation called upon to face it.
Many of these men should not have been in the military, much less in combat, in the first place. It is hard to see why they should be punished any
more—or any longer—than they already have been.

Policy Recommendations on the Vietnam Offender

Based on the analyses conducted in Chapters Two through Five, the following recommendations are made with respect to the men who hold less-
than-honorable discharges for absence offenses. These policy recommendations are alternatives and are placed in order of preference.

1. All absence-offense-related less-than-honorable discharges should be
subject to an immediate upgrade. The factors of race and class, the political climate in which these discharges were received, and the "life sentence"
nature of discharges dictate that new discharge papers should be issued
to prevent discrimination against these veterans. Once their discharges are
upgraded, these veterans should receive veterans benefits commensurate
with their time in service and duties performed *prior* to their offense.

2. If this first suggestion should be rejected, special categories of
Vietnam-era veterans should have their discharges upgraded on a class-by-
class basis. Conditions of service which might be taken into account in such
an amelioration of the present situation are Vietnam service, Project 100,000
membership, and time during the war when service was rendered. Such a
class-by-class upgrading would not only be more in keeping with the findings of this research, but would be more economical and less bureaucrati-
cally burdensome than any case-by-case approach.

The perspective of viewing military service and avoidance outcomes
as contingent on how a young man made a series of choices when facing
conscription and military service forms the basis for the analyses which

follow in Chapters Six and Seven. Desertion and going into exile were perhaps the worst strategies available for escaping service in the Second Indochina War. In order to appreciate this, it will be useful to examine at this point how the draft and military personnel systems worked during the period of the war.

6

Processes of Legal Avoidance: The Selective Service System

When President Ford's Clemency Board set about granting clemency to Vietnam-era draft offenders, Department of Defense and Department of Justice records estimated the eligible population of civilian offenders (convicted and fugitive) at a little over thirteen thousand persons. Only an estimated five percent of these young men had fled to a foreign country.[1] Since then it has been argued that the population of potential offenders is much greater due to non-registrations which for the most part went unrecorded.[2] Still, all estimates of those who actually broke the law to avoid conscription are relatively small compared to the Vietnam generation as a whole. This chapter will focus on the remainder of that cohort of males who faced the draft during the Vietnam period.

First, the chapter will examine the extent to which males who were not labeled as "draft resisters" sought to avoid military service in general and conscripted military service in particular. It will seek to delineate patterns of avoidance behavior and attempt to place these patterns within their social context with the ultimate goal of constructing a model of draft resistance and military service. In addition, it will examine the workings of the selective service classification system and the lottery. Finally, an effort will be made to gauge the effect that their experiences with the selective service system had on the consciousness of this generation of American men, of whom so many were caught in a dilemma between demands of the state and the goals of self.

Patterns of Avoidance

What were the means by which young men attempted to avoid being drafted into military service during the Second Indochina War? The Notre

Dame Survey specifically asked respondents whether or not they attempted to avoid conscription through a number of popularly conceived methods of escape. Since for convenience, each of these variables is assigned a shortened label in the following discussion, these labels and the original questions are listed below.

Label	Survey Question
Late Registration	When did you register for the draft? (1) I registered for the draft on time, right around my 18th birthday. (2) I registered late. (3) I never registered for the draft. (Answers (2) and (3) were considered attempts to avoid conscription by avoiding initial contact with the conscription bureaucracy.)
Learning	Did you try to learn as much as you could about ways to avoid the draft?
Expert Counseling	Did you ever talk with a lawyer or anyone else who was an expert on the draft?
Application	Did you ever apply directly to your draft board for a deferment or exemption?
School	Did the draft ever affect the time you spent in school? (1) Yes, it led me to go to school when I wouldn't otherwise have gone at all. (2) Yes, it kept me in school when I would have taken some time off from school. (3) Yes, I had to take more courses than I would have, in order to keep my deferment. (4) No, the draft did not affect my experience in school (Answers (1), (2), and (3) were all considered altering educational behavior in an attempt to avoid conscription.)
Marriage	Did you get married earlier than you would have because of your draft status?
Children	Did you have any children earlier than you would have because of your draft status?
Career	Was your career or choice of jobs ever influenced by your desire to avoid the draft?

Doctor	Did you ever talk to a doctor to try to get a physical exemption?
Mutilate	Did you ever do anything to your body to try to get a physical exemption?
Other	Aside from the ways already mentioned, did you ever try to change your personal circumstances to qualify for a draft exemption or deferment?
More	Beyond what you've already noted, did you do anything else to avoid the draft? (The three preceding questions requested details in the case of "yes" answers.)

Table 6-1 presents the frequency at which each of these types of draft resistance behavior were reported by the respondents in the Notre Dame Survey.

Since the mean total number of affirmative answers is 1.6, it becomes possible to suggest on the basis of this sample that the average American draft-eligible male committed between one and two attempts to avoid the draft during the Vietnam period. This statement is misleading in that forty-two percent of the Notre Dame respondents declared that they "in general" did not try to avoid the draft. Among those who did attempt to avoid, the average number of stated attempts was 2.3. That multiple attempts were common is also confirmed by looking at the relationship among these different avoidance strategies. Most of the relationships among the avoidance strategies are positive and significant, further supporting the hypothesis that individuals who attempt to avoid the draft by one means are more

Table 6-1.   **Draft Avoidance Behaviors (NDS)**

	Number of Respondents Reporting Behavior	Number of Respondents Answering	Percent
Late registration	233	1556	15
Learning	559	1553	36
Expert counseling	421	1561	27
Application	605	1551	39
School	399	1535	26
Marriage	47	1563	3
Children	31	1565	2
Career	161	1463	11
Doctor	320	1524	21
Mutilation	60	1501	4
Other	91	1521	6
More	150	1495	10

likely to attempt to avoid by some other means. The pattern is not quite that simple, however. If only very significant relationships are considered, three variables seem to be exceptions to the above statement. These are late registration, marriage, and children. Registering late, though pursued as a strategy by fifteen percent of the men in the Notre Dame Survey, is not significantly associated with any other method of draft avoidance. Getting married and having children to avoid the draft are very highly associated with one another and each, to a lesser extent, with going to school and choosing a draft-deferred career. Next there is a set of variables including learning about the draft, seeking expert counseling, applying for deferments, going to school, consulting a doctor, self-mutilation, "other," and "more" for which a square correlation matrix would contain only positive coefficients significant at the .001 level of significance. Career choice could have been included in this grouping if it were not for the fact that there is no significant relationship between choosing a draft-deferred occupation and altering one's body in an effort to escape conscription (6-2).

In summary, there seem to have been several groups of men pursuing different *sets* of strategies for avoiding the draft. The first group pursued a simple strategy consisting of one act, attempting to defer registration. The second attempted to escape conscription by getting married and having children while also seeking student and occupational deferments. A third group pursued a multiplicity of strategies ranging from getting legal assistance to self-mutilation and other forms of behavior not cited by the questionnaire. Finally, there are two more groups — one of which was willing to attempt anything besides self-mutilation and the other which opted for self-mutilation as a single strategy (6-4).

Efficiency of Draft Avoidance Behavior

One of the most crucial factors involved in an analysis of draft avoidance is the degree to which such behavior assisted an individual in avoiding military service. There were three possible outcomes for the draft-eligible man who wanted to avoid conscription; he could be drafted, he could enlist to escape being drafted, or he could escape military service altogether. For the time being, the focus will be on whether a man eventually performed military service.

It is clear that there are two basic categories of draft avoidance behaviors. There are those which significantly lessened an individual's chances of military service and those which had no effect whatsoever. The five avoidance behaviors which were apparently the most successful routes to non-service were learning as much as possible about the draft, obtaining expert legal counseling, simply applying for a deferment, seeing a doctor for expert medical counseling, and self-mutilation. In the preceding section, it was noted that these strategies were all significantly related to one another (6-2).

Late registration, which was found to be a strategy usually attempted in isolation, neither helped nor hurt persons attempting to avoid serving in the military. Marriage and having children, two significantly related strategies, were equally useless ways to avoid military service. More surprisingly, going to school and choosing a draft-deferrable career were in general demonstrably poor strategies for the overall population in the Notre Dame Survey. Going to a trade school, junior college, or college in order to avoid the draft did work for some young men, but in many other cases the close monitoring of school records by the Selective Service must have taken its toll in conscriptions and forced enlistments.[3] In other words, a young man who could do well in his studies and keep up his grade point average was better off in school, while a young man with a lack of academic skills placed himself "under the gun" by staking his chances of being drafted on his grade point average. The additional variables "other" and "more" which represent more than anything else the multiplicity of extremes to which men would go to avoid military service are also found to be unrelated to actual military service. Finally, attempting multiple strategies was more effective than trying a single method of avoiding military service (6-3).

In the appendix, a confirmatory principle components analysis of the ten major variables shows that there existed four pronounced patterns of avoidance behavior in the Notre Dame sample. Two of them evidently worked as a means of avoiding the draft. The other two did not. An effective multiple strategy involved learning about the draft, consulting a doctor, an expert counselor, or both, and applying for deferments. Not so appealing, but also effective was the single strategy of self-mutilation. Ineffective but usually tried together were getting married and having children. Failing to register or registering late was an ineffective strategy usually pursued by itself (6-4). The next question is, Who pursued each of these strategies?

The Social Context of Resistance

Included in the Notre Dame Survey were a limited number of social demographic items which can be expected to shed some light on the background and present conditions of the young men who attempted to avoid the draft in the ways already discussed. Among the background variables included there and considered here were race, family stability, father's military service, parents' attitude toward the draft, family's socioeconomic status, and the respondent's attitude toward the war when he faced the draft. Also included in the Notre Dame Survey were questions concerning the respondent's age and education. Two other variables considered in this analysis in addition to the twelve avoidance strategies already noted are the total number of the five successful strategies pursued by a respondent.

That there are indeed social forces at work in the selection of draft avoidance-strategies is revealed by the fact that certain of the social background variables discussed in previous chapters are significantly related to specific draft avoidance behaviors. Nonwhites were more likely to have registered late, a strategy already shown to be of little worth. Whites were more likely to pursue the not necessarily successful strategy of going to school, as well as the dubious strategies listed under "other" and "more." The very useful avoidance behaviors of applying for deferments and seeing doctors were much more likely to be reported by whites, and whites were somewhat more likely to seek expert counseling. Over all, the whites in the Notre Dame Survey are shown to be more likely to have pursued a greater number of draft avoidance behaviors than nonwhites (6-5).

Two of the background variables in the Notre Dame Survey—the presence of both natural parents in the home and father's military service—bear little or no positive relation to draft avoidance behavior. The significant *negative* relation between late registration and two natural parents in the home can in part be explained by the interrelations among race, socioeconomic status, and late registration and two natural parents in the home.

Sometimes the absence of significant relationships is just as interesting as their presence. The nonrelationship between the father's military service and the occurrence of most draft avoidance behavior reflects the degree to which a son's chances of resisting the draft are not affected by his father's military service even in a sample where sixty-three percent of all fathers served (6-4).

In another respect, however, parents' behavior did affect a son's reaction to the draft in a significant way. If parents encouraged a son to avoid getting drafted, he was, in fact, significantly more likely to do so (6-5). Not only was he somewhat more apt to go to school to avoid conscription, but he was much more likely to have pursued one of the five best strategies for escaping the draft. This finding supports the arguments of those students of socialization who have maintained that much of the rebellion in the late sixties was not the result of parent-offspring disagreement, but just the opposite, of offspring carrying through on parental values.[4]

The socioeconomic status (SES) of a respondent's family was recorded by the following question:

What was your family's economic situation when you were 18 years old?
(1) Poverty level.
(2) Working class.
(3) Middle class.
(4) Upper middle class.
(5) Wealthy.

This is what is normally referred to as a measure of "subjective" social class as distinguished from more preferred measures of social class based on occupation, education, and income. In American society, there is a tendency for everyone to think that he is a member of the middle class, thereby reducing the variance in a measure of subjective social class. Still, there is enough variance in responses to the Notre Dame Survey's SES item to produce some significant relationships between this item and the types of avoidance behavior. The lower an individual's social class the more likely he was to have tried late registration. This relationship indicates the class-defined nature of this almost worthless strategy. Individuals of higher socioeconomic status were somewhat more likely to go to school in order to avoid conscription and a little less likely to try marriage. However, more important are the significant relationships between SES and four of the draft avoidance strategies. Learning about the draft, seeking expert counseling, making applications, and consulting a doctor — four of the five most successful strategies — are associated with higher socioeconomic status (6-5).

One conclusion is very clear. Resisting the draft could lead to successful avoidance of military service if a young man chose the correct avoidance strategies. The most successful strategies were more likely to be chosen by those from a higher class background and less likely to be chosen by poor and working class youths.

Among the individuals who applied to President Ford's Clemency Board as a result of draft offenses, seventy-two percent mentioned either religious, political, or ethical objections to the war in Vietnam as motivating their offense. In the Notre Dame Sample, eighty-eight percent of the respondents stated that during the time they faced the draft they either opposed or had mixed feelings about the war. Avoiding the draft was not limited to only those young men who simply had misgivings about the war. The men who pursued most of the avoidance strategies were more likely to be opposed to the war. Worthy of note is the fact that the Notre Dame Survey respondents who were in favor of the war were just as likely to register late, have children to avoid conscription, choose a draft-deferred career, and physically alter their bodies as those who did not favor the war. Still, it is ironic that those individuals who were in favor of the war, but attempted to avoid the draft, did not choose very effective strategies in order to do so.

The respondent's age can provide one especially important piece of information. It allows this analysis to infer which draft avoidance behaviors were associated with which period within the Second Indochina War. When the war first began, most public opinion polls registered a general enthusiasm for it. By 1968 this trend had been reversed, with the war being considered a major factor in the erosion of support for Lyndon Johnson's presidency. The last few years of the war represented a steady deterioration of both public and military morale with respect to the war effort. Statistics involving age allow the correlation of service-avoidance techniques with this growing dissatisfaction. For instance, the fact that age in the Notre Dame Survey is not significantly related to late registration allows the suggestion that this means of avoidance was not associated with any particular phase in the war. On the other hand, the significant negative relation between age and learning about the draft makes it possible to suggest that as the war wore on more young men began to learn as much as possible about the workings of the conscription process. Earlier in the war, men were more prone to rely on applying for deferments, going to school, getting married, having children, and choosing a career as a means of escaping the draft. Later in the war, there is evidence that men began to turn increasingly to expert counseling and a combination of other more effective methods of avoidance (6-6).

The relationships between education and the draft avoidance behaviors are as expected. The higher a person's educational attainment, the less likely he is to have attempted to pursue an ineffective avoidance strategy such as late registration. More highly educated men were more likely to have used such effective draft avoidance behaviors as learning about the draft, seeking expert counseling, applying for deferments, and consulting a physician, as well as choosing a deferrable career. It is, of course, expected that those who attended school in order to avoid getting drafted would have a higher level of education at the time of the study. Perhaps, the ineffectiveness of going to school as a strategy accounts for the fact that the relationship between this strategy and education level actually attained is not as strong as that between some of the other strategies and that variable (6-6). In other words, men who pursued the singular strategy of going to school were not much more likely to avoid the draft and could have probably gotten more years of education by pursuing a more effective draft avoidance strategy while going to school simply to get an education.

The Draft Classification System

In addition to providing insight into how young men attempted to avoid being inducted into military service, the Notre Dame Survey also allows, to some extent, an analysis of how the Selective Service System worked during the Second Indochina War. Given a list of the most common types of draft exemptions which were available through selective service, each respondent was asked whether or not he had ever held a particular type deferment. For each type, he was allowed to answer yes, no, or not sure. "Not sures" are excluded from this analysis.

An analysis of eight common draft classifications shows that the fate of a young man in the selective service's classification system had very much to do with whether or not he entered military service. Men who had ever held a 1-A classification indicating availability for service were much more apt to have also performed military service. Men who had ever received one of six kinds deferments including student, graduate, hardship, occupational, physical, or mental or who had been classified as a conscientious objector were significantly less likely to have performed military service. Though a classification of 1-A was not permanent and very often could be changed, the significant relationship between performing military service and ever having held the 1-A classification indicates that military-phobic men were quite justified in taking such a classification seriously. Although the relationships between the different draft exemptions are all significant at the one in a thousand level, it is still possible to speculate on the basis of their relative magnitudes as to which classifications were more likely to protect their bearers from military service. The safest bets for the avoider were very clearly the student deferment, if one could be obtained, and the physical exemption (6-7).

Once again the age of respondents is used as an indicator of the shifting situation during the Vietnam period. This is easily illustrated in the case of the graduate student deferment, which was eventually eliminated. The older respondents who faced the draft early in the war are significantly more likely to have had a graduate student deferment simply because it was not available to the younger respondents who faced the draft nearer the end of the war. Some deferments such as the student deferment and the conscientious objector status remained equally as available (or unavailable) throughout the duration of the conflict. Hardship deferments, occupational deferments, and medical exemptions were more commonly obtained early in the war, but men who faced the draft earlier in the war were also more likely to be classified 1-A, since the demand for personnel was greatest then. With the passage of time there was an increased chance of "slipping" into the 1-A category even if a man had earlier received another classification (6-7).

One questionnaire item asked the Notre Dame Survey respondents if they were consciously trying to avoid the draft. The individuals who admitted such conscious avoidance were more likely than others to have obtained student, graduate student, and conscientious objector deferments.

Two deferments which are most clearly linked to the social class of respondents are the student and the graduate student deferments. Such deferments were, according to the Notre Dame Survey, more likely to be held by those who were white, whose parents encouraged them to avoid the draft, who tried to avoid the draft, and whose family was perceived by them as belonging to a higher social class. They were also less likely to be in favor of the war. Not surprisingly, these deferments are highly correlated with greater education.

Absent are indications that nonwhites were more likely than whites to be classified 1-A, and there is only a very mild negative correlation between family's social class and the 1-A classification. The weakness of this correlation may in fact be explained by a tendency of lower-class men to enlist in response to the appeal of military service as a route to economic stability or as a last resort to escape an unsatisfactory niche in the social order. Evidence of racial or class discrimination in the granting of conscientious objector status is likewise missing. Of course, this could have been a result of the close relationship between this classification and membership in legitimate "pacifist" religions.

The Lottery

With the Nixon administration's ascent to power, a new dimension was added to the conscription process. Every nineteen-year-old and college-deferred male suddenly had a number attached to his birthdate through the process of a national lottery. One question asked of the Notre Dame Sample was, "Was your lottery number high enough to enable you to avoid the draft?"

Examining the relationships between answering "Yes" to the lottery question and other variables in the study reveals a number of significant correlations (6-8). In addition to the significant negative relationship between a perceived "high" lottery number and military service is a rather strong positive relationship between a "Yes" answer and having had a student deferment.

There have been suggestions that the distribution of lottery numbers over the days of the year was biased against those men born in January and February and in favor of those who already had student deferments.[5] Although the former hypothesis can be statistically verified, why the latter should be true is not obvious, and requires careful analysis. The capacity for testing it here is limited by the nature of the question asked.

The question solicits the *perception* of the respondent, and it is likely that the respondents' perceptions may have varied with their social class or with their situation relative to the draft. Many lower-class individuals may simply not have kept up with lottery cutoff numbers, which varied geographically from year to year. A substantial portion of the Vietnam generation who were already on active duty would have randomly received numbers that were obviously high — without affecting their military status. Similarly, many older men, having already escaped military service in some other way, would not have perceived their lottery number as having helped them.

Men, on the other hand, who already had student deferments at the time of the lottery had one advantage over their nondeferred counterparts: they could keep their deferments until they finished their courses of study. For men graduating in 1971 or 1972, for example, this would have meant that they would have become eligible for the draft closer to the end of the war, when the numbers of men being drafted were decreasing. Thus their student deferments would have made them less likely to serve — and more likely to report having "high" numbers.

Individuals with student deferments had a further advantage in that they could, if they chose, in any given year drop their student deferments and be considered for the draft in that year, with their lottery numbers assigned from previous lotteries. As an illustration, suppose a nineteen-year-old college sophomore received a lottery number of 150 in the first year's drawing, in 1969. When he heard a projection that the highest number drafted that year through his local board was estimated to be 160, he would naturally keep his deferment. But when the next year's projected cutoff number was, say, 130, he could exercise his option, drop his student deferment, become eligible for and escape the draft — and thus be beyond the reach of the Selective Service System. And he would have responded to the question on the Notre Dame Survey with a "Yes." His number was high enough to enable him to avoid the draft. At the same time, other men with the same birthdate — and hence identical lottery numbers of 150 — but without student deferments would have been drafted in their first year of eligibility, and would have answered the survey question with a "No."

This "loophole" alone could account for the significant association between having a college deferment and having a lottery number high enough to avoid the draft. This association is also strong enough to account for the relationships between high-lottery-number "escapees" and being white, better educated, and from a higher social class background, since all these variables have already been shown to be related to getting the student deferment in the first place.

The Attitudinal Residue

What effect did their experiences with the operation of the selective service system during the Vietnam period have on the consciousness of the young men who participated in the Notre Dame Survey? How fair did they feel was this process which had such an impact on their formative years? How did their experience affect their attitude towards the United States government? The following questions were included on the Notre Dame Survey.

Label	Survey Question
Draft Fair	If you were to describe the way your draft board treated you, would you say it was very fair, basically fair, somewhat unfair, or very unfair?
Draft Fair to Friends	If you were to describe the way your draft board treated your friends, would you say it was very fair, basically fair, somewhat unfair, or very unfair? (Coded similarly to Draft Fair.)
Respondent Favored War	Which of the following was your position towards the war when you faced the draft? (1) I thought the war was right. (2) I had mixed feelings about the war. (3) I thought the war was wrong. (Those who felt the war was "right"

are coded as one, and those who felt the war was "wrong" or had mixed feelings were coded as zero.)

Now Favors War

Which of the following is your position towards the war?

Attitude Towards Government

Would you say that your experience with the draft system has affected your general attitude towards the government favorably, unfavorably, or not at all?

Avoid More

If you had it to do over again, would you have tried to avoid serving in the military any more or any less than you actually did?
(1) I would have tried harder to avoid serving in the military.
(2) I would have done about what I actually did.
(3) I would not have tried as hard to avoid serving in the military.

The social psychological theory of cognitive dissonance suggests that attitudes in the human mind work towards a degree of "balance." If this is true, a person's antagonistic attitudes tend to be resolved or forgotten and a degree of cognitive uniformity maintained.[6] For this reason, some conservatism must be used when interpreting a set of questions about what a person thought at some previous time in his life. Robert Merton's "self-fulfilling prophecy" is an additional complicating factor in that what a person expects to experience will often be experienced.[7]

Most of the relationships among the survey variables are as might be expected. Those who felt the draft was fair to them also felt it was fair to their friends, and those who felt it was unfair to themselves felt that it was similarly unfair to their friends. Respondents' attitudes towards the war had not changed significantly since the years in which they faced conscription. Those who felt the draft was fair were more likely to have felt more favorably toward the government as a result of their selective service experiences, while those who regarded their treatment as unfair had taken a more unfavorable attitude towards their government. Finally, a person's assessment of the draft's fairness was a function of his attitude towards the war when he was of draft eligible age (6-9).

The relationships between each of the attitudes and other variables may also be of interest. Once again the phase of the war during which an individual faced the draft, incorporated in the respondent's age, is shown to be important in several ways. Older men who faced the draft earlier in the war are more likely to feel the draft treated their friends fairly, to have favored the war then and now, and to have an enhanced attitude toward the government as a result of their draft experience. Younger men are more likely to exhibit the opposite opinions (6-10).

Whites are more likely than nonwhites to have considered their draft board's treatment of them and their friends to have been fair. A more unfavorable attitude toward the government was expressed by those men whose parents had urged them to avoid getting drafted. The well-educated and men from lower class families are more likely to have developed increased hostility toward their government as a result of their selective service experiences. Interestingly enough, men who were actually drafted tend to express doubts about the fairness of their treatment by the draft. The only group to show a significant decrease in their positive sentiments toward the war between their draft eligibility and the present are those who served in the military in the interim. Overall, it is safe to conclude that the background characteristics and draft experiences of men had diverse effects on their attitudes toward the selective service system and government it represented (6-10), (6-11), (6-12).

Summary

The interaction of men with limited sets of avoidance behavior and the workings of the Selective Service System has been the subject of this chapter. The interview schedule of the Notre Dame Survey of the Vietnam Generation gave respondents a chance to indicate whether they had attempted to avoid the draft in several legal ways. Analysis revealed that well-defined groups of men had pursued similar sets of strategies.

Certain of these strategy sets were shown to be related to successfully avoiding military service, while others were not. Successful strategies were more likely to have been chosen by white, upper-class men with more years of educational achievement. Preferable (in terms of not having to perform military service) draft classifications were similarly distributed in the sample. Attitudes toward the conscription process and the government were related to race and actual experiences with the draft and military during the war.

From the institutional perspective, the conscription process brought onto active duty those categories of men who were least suitable to military service. The poor and members of minorities were those who were less likely to choose the strategies most likely to enable a man to escape military service. Men who had the greatest potential for integration into complex organizations were more likely to escape to the nonmilitary organizations in the society.

In the case of avoiding the draft, an individual's choices of action were found to have a significant influence on his social outcomes. This perfectly coincides with the purposive actor model of behavior in which an individual's fate is determined by his rational decisions on how to best achieve his goals. The limits of this model are defined by the significant relationship between how a man chooses to act and his social background.

An examination of the importance of resources to the strategies available highlights the role of social class in effective draft avoidance. Two of the most successful strategies — consulting a doctor or a lawyer — were options not easily followed by members of minorities and lower class people in general. For individuals with economic resources or the right social connections, the advice of doctors and lawyers was more readily available. Even learning as much as possible about the conscription process was a feat which was more easily accomplished when in possession of educational resources unavailable to lower-class individuals.

Avoidance behavior more commonly available to everyone in American society, such as getting married and having children, did not exhibit any correlation with class nor any special effectiveness as means of avoiding military service. It does not take much sociological imagination to envision two different scenarios for self-mutilation: the upper-class youth consulting a sympathetic physician (note the significant correlation between these two techniques) for some refined "safe" method of altering his body and the lower class youth more dangerously attempting self-mutilation on his own devices.

It is important to note that the social class model of draft avoidance leaves much to probability so that some middle and upper class males eventually came to face military service as an inevitability. Once this stage in the process was reached, what further options were available to the man who wanted to gain his veterans benefits and at the same time avoid being assigned to Indochina? The next step in the process of surviving the Vietnam era will be explored in Chapter Seven.

7

Processes of Legal Avoidance:
The Military Personnel Structure

The draft became an obsession among American males during the late sixties and early seventies. The possibilities which faced these young men seemed clearcut. On one side were the dangers of combat in the steamy milieu of Indochina; on the other, the luxuries and advantages associated with a booming economy. In reality, this view of contrasting opportunities is a complete caricature. First, despite an overall appearance of abundance in American life during this period, there were still young men for whom civilian status was not a world of endless opportunities. Secondly, not all the young men who served on active duty in the armed forces during this period were assigned to combat duty in Indochina.

This chapter will focus only on the degree to which men who served in the armed forces during the Second Indochina War sought to avoid service in Vietnam. The relevance of such an analysis to the question of amnesty for draft avoiders and military absence offenders should be made clear. Previous analyses have shown those who deserted from military service during the Vietnam war to be, as were deserters in previous wars, men from lower socioeconomic backgrounds with educations well below the national average and frequently with no strong opinions on the war whatsoever. It will be suggested here that the young men who were labeled as deserters may have exhibited the only type of avoidance behavior of which they had an awareness. The previous chapter on legal forms of draft avoidance demonstrated that other young men, more well integrated into the institutional fabric of American life, were also attempting to avoid the responsibilities of military service. This chapter will carry the process one step further by producing evidence of the degree to which members of the armed forces who did not desert employed more complicated legally-sanctioned behavior to avoid Vietnam service.

Of the 1566 men who participated in the Notre Dame Survey of the Vietnam Generation, 572 served in the military during the Second Indochina War. It is this portion of the Notre Dame sample with which this chapter will be concerned.

Patterns of Personnel Policy Manipulation

Each branch of the armed services constitutes a large self-contained bureaucracy, the operation of which is contingent upon a labyrinth of rules and regulations. The fate of an individual within a branch of the armed forces is very often a result of the degree to which he understands and masters this body of rules and regulations. In the Notre Dame Survey there are seven questions which relate to ways in which respondents could have legally used the personnel policy structure of the military to avoid Vietnam service. These are listed below.

Label	*Survey Question*
Postponed Service	Once you realized that you were likely to be drafted, did you try to postpone your active military service?
Enlisted in Low Involvement Branch	At the time you entered the service, did you enlist in a branch of the service which you thought would reduce your chances of going to Vietnam?
Enlisted in Low Risk MOS	At the time you entered the service, did you enlist in an occupational specialty which you thought would not involve combat?
Change to Low Risk MOS	After you were in the service, did you change your occupational specialty in a way which reduced your chances of going to Vietnam?
Volunteer Long-term Low-risk Assignment	Once you were in the military, did you ever volunteer for a long-term military assignment that reduced your risk of going to Vietnam?
In-service CO Application	Did you ever apply for in-service conscientious objector once you were in the military?
Other	Once you were in the military did you ever do anything other than what is described above to avoid having to go to Vietnam? (Specific details were requested with "yes" answers to this question.)

Among those in the Notre Dame Survey who served in the armed forces, forty-eight percent stated that they had to some extent tried to avoid going to Vietnam. The degree to which these men relied on the foregoing strategies is shown in Table 7-1. Three ways of attempting to avoid Vietnam service were especially common. All of these—postponing active duty, enlisting for a branch which lessened the possibility of going to Vietnam, and enlisting for a noncombat occupational specialty—involved actions taken prior to going on active duty. The other four avoidance behaviors, which were less likely to be used, were available once an individual had entered active service. The least common procedure for avoiding Vietnam or combat once on active duty was the in-service conscientious objector application. Furthermore, seven percent of the veterans in the Notre Dame sample admit going beyond the six most well-known procedures for using the military personnel system to avoid Vietnam service. A host of more esoteric regulations beyond the knowledge or ingenuity of the average serviceman were manipulated by these men.

The average number of attempts to use personnel procedures to escape Vietnam service is 1.6 for those who made such attempts. According to the Notre Dame Survey, as many as forty-eight percent of the men who were on active duty during the Second Indochina War made between one and two attempts to avoid going to Vietnam by utilizing available procedural options.

In examining legal draft avoidance behaviors, definite patterns of multiple avoidance emerged. These can be examined by studying the bivariate relationships between each pair of Vietnam avoidance behaviors. As with draft avoidance behaviors, significant positive relationships are the rule. The strongest relationships are (1) between enlisting for a low-involvement branch and enlisting for a low-risk occupational specialty and (2) between

Table 7-1.   **Vietnam Assignment Avoidance Behaviors: Frequencies Reported in Notre Dame Survey**

	Number of Respondents Reporting Behavior	Number of Respondents Answering	Percent
Postponed service	157	530	30
Enlisted in low-involvement branch	136	547	25
Enlisted in low-risk MOS	152	550	28
Changed to low-risk MOS	57	552	10
Volunteer long-term low-risk assignment	68	555	12
In-service CO application	15	553	3
Other	36	540	7

volunteering for a long-term low-risk assignment and changing to a low-risk occupational specialty. Special "package deals" offered by recruiters and reenlistment NCOs are probably responsible for the high correlation between each of these pairs of variables (7-2).

Otherwise, most of the correlations of interest are those which are not significant. For example, individuals who enlisted in low-involvement branches were not as likely as others to apply for changes in occupational specialties once they were on active duty. At the same time, men who had enlisted for a low-risk occupational specialty were more likely than those who did not to apply for an even safer MOS once they were on active duty. In-service conscientious objector applications were rare among those who postponed military service or enlisted in a low-involvement branch, but such applications were more common among those who enlisted for a low-risk occupational specialty and much more common among those who also employed one of the other three in-service methods for avoiding going to Vietnam. Most who postponed active duty did not resort to the wide variety of personnel escape routes encompassed by the variable "other," while those routes were more likely to be taken by men who had already attempted one of the other five types of Vietnam-avoidance behaviors (7-2).

Effectiveness of Vietnam Avoidance Behavior

As with draft avoidance behaviors, the big question involved in attempts to avoid Vietnam service through manipulating the personnel structure of the armed forces is the degree to which strategies were effective. This can be seen by examining the relationships between each of the personnel strategies for avoiding Vietnam and whether the individual choosing such strategies actually served there. For those who did go to Vietnam, it may also be important to gain some idea of the degree to which an individual who had employed any of the personnel strategies was more likely to avoid combat once assigned to Vietnam.

In observing the relationships between personnel strategies for avoidance, it is possible to discern two major clusters of personnel avoidance behaviors. There are first those which were employed at the time of or prior to induction, such as postponing active duty, enlisting in a safer branch, and enlisting in a safer MOS. In contrast with these three pre-service or "early" strategies, there are three post-induction or "later" strategies, which include changing to a safer MOS, volunteering for a long-term, low-risk assignment, and applying for in-service conscientious objector status. These two clusters of strategies in reality correspond to those which worked and those which did not (7-3).

The three early strategies are all negatively related to Vietnam service at a significant level, indicating that those men who bargained with the military personnel structure's representatives at time of enlistment were significantly less likely to go to Vietnam. In cases where these early attempts to manipulate the personnel system failed, and an individual was sent to Vietnam anyway, early bargainers are shown to have been significantly less likely to see combat (7-4).

Later bargainers were not nearly so fortunate in their attempts to avoid Vietnam service; and having failed to avoid Vietnam service, those who changed to a safer MOS or volunteered for a long-term low-risk assignment were no more likely to avoid combat. Those men who attempted to find other loopholes in the personnel system were only somewhat more likely to avoid Vietnam and once there no more likely to avoid combat. The in-service conscientious objector applicants constitute a special case. They were no more likely to avoid Vietnam, but once assigned to Vietnam, they were more likely to avoid combat (7-4).

Finally, by creating the variable "total personnel manipulation" — which is simply the sum of all of the ways a man attempted to manipulate the personnel structure to avoid Vietnam and combat — it is possible to show that individuals who displayed more tenacity and determination in dealing with the military personnel system were significantly more likely to avoid Vietnam service. The attempt to avoid Vietnam failing, these more frequent manipulators were still less likely to see combat while stationed in Indochina (7-4).

The Social Context of Personnel Manipulation

As previously mentioned, an article on Vietnam casualties suggested that the significant relationships between casualty levels and social class might be a function of the degree to which individuals of higher class backgrounds are more competent at coping with the personnel structures of formal organizations.[1] To a certain extent this greater competency is reflected in higher scores on standardized tests; but how well one fares at the hands of bureaucratic machinery is very often a matter of how well one can fill out forms and master the intricate sets of rules by which such bureaucracies operate.[2] With respect to military service, this last factor is reflected in the degree to which an individual is confident and effective in dealing with the personnel structure to achieve his desired ends.

To what extent does each of the personnel manipulation strategies relate to the variables in social background? Some variables, such as race, natural family, and father's service record have little association with any of the personnel manipulation variables. Whites were slightly more likely to have postponed service and enlisted in a safer branch, both effective means of avoiding Vietnam service and combat. The number of ways in which a respondent attempted to escape Vietnam and combat service is mildly related to the presence of both natural parents in the home, as it is to father's having served in the military (7-5).

As with draft avoidance behavior, parents' attitudes toward the son's military service is shown to be an important variable with respect to a respondent's attempts to avoid Vietnam and combat by taking advantage of personnel structure options. Parents' encouragement to avoid being drafted is significantly related to a respondent's pursuing any of the three pre-service bargaining strategies and to the number of personnel manipulation strategies pursued overall. This is all the more important due to the significant negative relationships these four variables bear to both Vietnam and combat service (7-4, 7-5).

The measure of subjective social class background is not nearly so important a factor in the manipulation of the military personnel structure as it was for draft avoidance. It was significantly related to the three pre-service manipulations, but it is slightly related to changing occupational specialties in a negative direction (7-5). This indicates that the higher a person's social class background, the less likely he was to pursue this ineffective means of avoiding Vietnam service.

An individual's own position on the American presence in Vietnam is revealed to have had a significant influence on the probability of his having attempted to avoid Vietnam and combat through manipulating the military personnel structure. Only volunteering for a long-term low-risk assignment is not significantly related to a respondent's attitude toward the war. A man's attitude toward the war is the background characteristic most closely associated with the total number of ways a man attempted to use the personnel structure to escape Vietnam service (7-5).

For the last two social demographic variables, age and education, significant correlations with the personnel manipulation variables are few. Younger men who faced the possibility of going to Vietnam later in the war are more likely to have tried a greater number of personnel manipulation strategies, showing some preference for enlisting in safe branches and occupational specialties and volunteering for long-term low-risk assignments. The three effective pre-service bargaining strategies were more likely to have been chosen by the better educated, while individuals with fewer years of education were more likely to volunteer for long-term low-risk assignments (7-5).

The Military Context of Personnel Manipulation

A dimension which did not exist in the case of draft avoidance behavior should be considered in examining personnel structure manipulation. The men in this part of the Notre Dame sample all served in the military, and it is not improbable that efforts to avoid Vietnam and combat service might be related to some of the conditions of that service. Relationships between personnel manipulation variables and three military career variables are, therefore, examined in this section.

It has been previously noted that just as many men in the Notre Dame sample enlisted to avoid being drafted as enlisted for other reasons. This analysis reveals that the men who eventually did get drafted were somewhat more likely than those who enlisted to attempt to postpone service. Otherwise, draftees were limited to and were more likely to take advantage of opportunities to change their military occupational specialties or volunteer for long-term, low-risk assignments. Neither of these have been shown to be significantly related to avoiding Vietnam service (7-6).

Individuals who served in the Army or Marines were considered to have belonged to the more risk-associated ground force. This makes it possible to examine whether men who belonged to these ground force branches of service were more or less prone to attempt to avoid Vietnam service than men in other branches. Being in the ground force services had little to do with the degree to which men manipulated the personnel structure to avoid going to Vietnam (7-6).

The last military career variable, time in service, bears little relation to most personnel manipulation practices. Time spent on active duty is negatively related to postponing service, enlisting in a safer branch, and pursuing "other" personnel procedures to avoid going to Vietnam. The second of these correlations is curious since enlistments in the Navy and Air Force exceeded those for the Army. A mild association between time in service and volunteering for a long-term, low-risk assignment is in the expected direction. Overall, though, military career variables are not as important as social background variables in predicting the likelihood of personnel structure manipulation and especially, effective manipulation.

Personnel Manipulation in Vietnam

Not all men assigned to Vietnam experienced combat. Previously it was shown that manipulation of the military personnel structure is significantly related to having avoided combat once assigned to Vietnam. This result can be interpreted in more than one way. It could mean that events prior to Vietnam service, such as an individual's successful bargaining with a recruiter, determine the probability of experiencing combat once the individual is assigned to Vietnam. On the other hand, since the total number of personnel manipulation strategies is negatively related to combat service, it is possible that personnel manipulation is an ongoing process. This suggests that early in his military career a serviceman developed a pattern of personnel manipulation and that it is this pattern of personnel manipulation which increased his chances of avoiding combat once he was assigned to Vietnam.

In the Notre Dame Survey, there are three items which can aid in choosing between these two theoretical possibilities. Concerning in-country personnel manipulation, they are as follows.

Label	Survey Question
Saigon	While in Vietnam, did you volunteer for an assignment in Saigon or another non-combat location?
Non-Combat Job	While in Vietnam, did you volunteer for a non-combat job assignment?
Reduce	While in Vietnam, did you do anything else to reduce your chances of having to engage in combat? (Specific details were requested with "yes" answers to this question.)

From examining the relationships among these variables, there is definitely a pattern of personnel structure manipulation which existed for persons assigned to Vietnam. From the significant positive relationships between the in-Vietnam types of personnel manipulation attempts, it is evident that an individual who tried one of these procedural means to avoid combat was more likely to have tried another. He was also more likely to have a history of personnel manipulation. Despite the existence of such a pattern, the important point is the general ineffectiveness of all three types of in-Vietnam attempts to avoid combat through manipulating the personnel structure. This finding, in combination with already stated findings, demonstrates that servicemen who hoped to avoid combat through manipulating the personnel structure had to have done so prior to being assigned to Vietnam. Once a man arrived in Long Binh or Cam Rahn Bay, his fate in the workings of the personnel structure were beyond the influence of his own actions (7-7).

Determinants of Personnel Manipulation and Vietnam Service

In a departure from the procedure used so far of treating only the relationship between any two variables at a time, it is useful to model the military careers of the members of Vietnam generation toward or away from Vietnam service as a causal process using multiple regression analysis (7-8, 7-9, 7-10).[3] The overview of this process can be seen in Figure 7-11.

The model includes three sets of variables arranged in a causal sequence over the life histories of the men involved. At the first level is the individual's social background which has its impact both directly and indirectly on whether or not he served in Vietnam. These social background variables directly affect a set of second level variables which are considered to be the individual's prerogatives at the time he faced the possibility of service. Finally, on the third level are the variables of the conditions of the individual's service which play their own significant role in the outcome of the overall process and which are, in part, determined by the two preceding levels of variables.

A description of the causal sequence which led to escape or service begins with the individual's social origin. Two of these social background conditions, age and race, retain their direct impact on Vietnam service even when all other variables are controlled. Age should be regarded as the cohort or year within the Vietnam generation when the man was born. All previous research on the Vietnam generation has emphasized the importance of this variable. Here, age has a significant direct impact on both the individual's attitude toward the war and whether or not he attempted to avoid the draft. White men were more likely to attempt to employ the more effective means for avoiding the war through personnel structure manipulation. Other social background factors which affected an individual's likelihood of effectively using the personnel structure include social class and parents' attitudes toward the war.

At the level of individual prerogatives, three variables figure significantly in the model of avoiding Vietnam service while on active duty. Effective manipulation of the personnel system was significantly affected by the other two individual prerogative variables, the individual's attitude toward the war and his history of dealing with the selective service system. Education, age, and parental attitudes about the draft all contributed in shaping the young man's attitude toward the war. These same three background variables and his attitude toward the war helped to determine whether or not the youth would attempt to avoid being drafted. If he had attempted to avoid being drafted, he was more likely to employ effective personnel structure manipulation to avoid assignment to the combat zone. Effective personnel structure manipulation was also more likely to occur as a result of the separate and direct impact of his opposition to the war. The social class of his family and the opposition of his parents to his being drafted also directly affected his willingness to wrestle with the bureaucratic intricacies of the personnel system.

The length of time which an individual spent on active duty and his assignment to the Army or the Marines Corps directly affected the likelihood that a man would go to Vietnam. His effective manipulation of the personnel structure had a significant effect on each of these conditions of service. Time in service was also directly affected by a young man's history of attempting to avoid the draft and his cohort within the Vietnam generation. Both his time in service and his branch assignment were significantly dependent on his level of education.

Vietnam service is, therefore, shown to be the outcome of a complex set of social conditions and decisions. The most important attribute of the model is the central location within the causal process of the individual's willingness to utilize the personnel system to avoid service in Vietnam. While the social conditions of a man's family of origin unfairly set the stage for the distribution of service among the members of the Vietnam generation, his own conscious choices with respect to attitude toward the war and action in the face of powerful corporate actors remained a crucial factor in whether or not he was sent to Vietnam.

The Attitudinal Residue

Finally, as with the young men who faced conscription during the Vietnam era, the Notre Dame Survey permits an analysis of the attitudinal results of military service during the Second Indochina War. Of the men in the sample who experienced active duty, the Notre Dame Survey asked the following questions.

Label	*Survey Question*
Military Fair	If you were to describe the way the military treated you, would you say it was very fair, basically fair, somewhat unfair, or very unfair?
Military Fair to Friends	If you were to describe the way the military treated your friends in the service, would you say it was very fair, basically fair, somewhat unfair, or very unfair?
Favorable Effect on Government Attitude	Would you say that your experience with the military has affected your general attitude towards the government favorably, unfavorably, or not at all?
Try Harder to Avoid Vietnam Service	If you had to do it over again, would you have tried to avoid going to Vietnam any more or any less than you actually did?
National Purpose	While you were in the military, did you think of yourself as serving an important national purpose?
Personal Benefit	Do you think you benefited personally from your experience in the military?

While bearing in mind the previously-stated qualifications regarding attitudinal questions, we may note here that the attitudes of respondents in the Notre Dame Survey are characterized by a considerable degree of congruity. All relationships between attitudes are significant and in the expected directions. Veterans who felt the military was fair to them are more likely to feel that the military was fair to their friends and are more likely to have experienced a favorable effect on their attitude towards the government as a result of their military service. Veterans who felt that the military treated them less than fairly are more likely to express negative attitudes toward the military on the other survey items (7-12).

The role of social background in shaping these attitudinal orientations is important. Once again, a respondent's chronological place in the Vietnam generation is a crucial factor, as is revealed by a significant relationship between each of the attitudinal variables and age. Older veterans are more likely to have found the military to be fair and to evaluate as positive its effect on their attitude toward the government. Younger veterans are more likely to respond in the opposite manner on each of these matters, including expressing doubts as to whether they were serving an important national purpose while on active duty. Only an individual's position on the war shows so ubiquitous a relationship to the six attitudinal variables. From these relationships, it is apparent that a man's approval or disapproval of the war at the time he was eligible for the draft influenced his subsequent reaction to military service (7-13).

A man's experience with the draft is significantly related to all the attitudinal variables except for his evaluation of the military's fairness to himself. It is interesting that a man who attempted to avoid the draft prior to military service is no more likely to feel that the military treated him unfairly, but he *is* more apt to feel that the military treated his friends unfairly (7-13). One explanation for this finding can be derived from the foregoing causal model of Vietnam service. There it was shown that a history of attempting to avoid the draft was a prime determinant of effective personnel manipulation. Since such mastery of institutional mechanisms proved to be useful in obtaining desirable outcomes with respect to both the selective service and military assignment processes, it is not unlikely that a practitioner of institutionally approved avoidance would consider his own "deal" from the military to be quite fair. His condemnation of the system's fairness is more likely to have stemmed from the experiences of less talented comrades. In the same vein, a man who had attempted to avoid the draft is more likely to have had his attitude toward the government affected negatively by his active duty experiences. Likewise, he is more likely to express an intent to avoid all the more diligently if he had it all to do over again, and he is more likely to see his military service as providing no national or personal benefits (7-13).

Whites compared to nonwhites are more likely to consider the military fair, and nonwhites are more prone to declare their intention to avoid more if they have it to do over again. Well-educated men are more likely to have had their attitude toward the government damaged by military service and are more likely to decry their active duty as serving no important national purpose. Perhaps the similar yet weaker relationships between these attitudes and perceived social class are a function of the relationship between education and social class. Parents' encouragement to avoid conscription is associated with a disbelief in the military's fairness, national purpose, and benefit to servicemen (7-13).

The conditions of military service exhibit relationships to several of the attitudinal variables treated in this section. Draftees are only slightly more disposed than enlistees to feel that they were treated unfairly by the military. They are significantly less likely, however, to feel that they personally benefited from their military experiences. While favorable responses on the attitude items are associated with time in service, it is especially noteworthy that this promilitary relationship does not hold across the board. Men who spent more time on active duty were less likely to admit that they would try harder to avoid Vietnam service if they had it to do over again (7-14).

Veterans who served in Vietnam are more disposed than their comrades to feel that their active duty fulfilled an important national purpose. The same holds for men who saw combat, when they are compared to other men who served in Vietnam. Still, the most telling finding is that those veterans who served in Vietnam had a greater tendency than others to say that they would try harder to avoid Vietnam if they had it to do over again. Despite the argument that men who did not serve in Vietnam would have no real reason to try harder to avoid such service, it is extremely interesting that men who have served in Vietnam should, when asked a hypothetical question, indicate a desire to have successfully avoided such service (7-14).

A nonsignificant relationship between the number of personnel manipulation strategies tried and the fairness of the military in dealing with the respondent supports a previous suggestion that successful personnel manipulators have little reason to complain concerning their own treatment by the military. That those who took advantage of structural options to avoid Vietnam service feel a generalized antipathy towards the military establishment is indicated by their answers to the other five attitudinal items. The positive relationship between a history of personnel manipulation and trying harder to avoid Vietnam service in a hypothetical situation is evidence that institutional avoiders would not only repeat their avoidance behavior but would increase it (7-14).

Summary

This examination of military personnel structure manipulation during the Vietnam period has sought to demonstrate the degree to which servicemen on active duty attempted through legal means to avoid serving in Vietnam or experiencing combat. The results are clear. A substantial number of the men who served in the armed forces during that period struggled through the personnel avenues at their disposal to avoid Vietnam. There were, in general, three patterns of such behavior. One group of men engaged in pre-induction bargaining. These men, who were more likely to be white, upper class, and well-educated, were less likely to experience Vietnam or combat. Another group of men engaged in post-induction bargaining with representatives of the military personnel structure. These servicemen were not significantly more likely to avoid Vietnam or combat service. Finally, a small proportion of men applied for in-service conscientious objector status. While these men were not less likely to be assigned to Vietnam, they were less likely to experience combat (7-4, 7-5, 7-6).

The social demographic background of men was shown to be less important in the incidence of personnel structure manipulation than such factors were shown to be in legal draft avoidance behavior. Perceived social class of a respondent's family, his parents' advice, his education, and his own position toward the war were revealed to be important in influencing his use of the most effective forms of personnel structure manipulation. The conditions of a man's military service seemed to have little to do with his attempts to manipulate the military personnel structure. In fact, a treatment of in-country attempts to avoid combat indicated that a serviceman's earliest dealings with the personnel structure, especially at the time of recruitment, were more important determinants of combat experience.

A Social Simulation

If a theorist were charged with modeling, in some comprehensible fashion, the process of service in the Second Indochina War, he might settle on a macabre simulation game for which the board would resemble the flow charts in Baskir and Strauss' *Chance and Circumstance*. This fits well with the purposive actor approach described in Chapter One. A purposive actor is an individual with a specific set of interests and a set of available actions or strategies which may or may not be effective for achieving his desired outcomes. His task is to select correctly the most effective strategies to reach his goal.

Chapter Six best illustrates the way the "game" worked with respect to military service. The interests of an actor are represented by his attitude toward the war and the draft. If a man were eager to serve, he had no problem. The avenues were open. If he were unwilling to avoid conscription, he could put himself in the hands of the system and trust in chance. The essence of the game involved those men who tried to avoid.

As was seen in the analysis, some strategies worked and some did not. Often complex combinations of strategies were the safest play.

Social circumstance determined a man's chances of winning by determining his mode of play. Men from higher class backgrounds chose the more effective strategy combinations. Men from lower class backgrounds chose less effective strategies. Losers moved on to the next stage of the game.

Avoiding Indochina service while performing active duty military service was not a bad outcome. The process for achieving this is described in Chapter Seven. Time was a complicating element at this stage of play. Post-induction strategies were consistently of little use. Again, however, social class and race are associated with a man's mode of play.

One of the worst post-induction strategies was going absent-without-leave. Class, race, and other social factors worked to define the outcomes in this sector of the game also.

Baskir and Strauss' choice of *Chance and Circumstance* as the title for their book can be seen as a good one on the basis of this theoretical model. The twist in focus here is that the game was not played by individuals but by social classes of men. Beyond the parts of the game not captured in the foregoing exposure is the incidence of casualty, the most serious outcome of all. The existent analyses of casualty rates show that this phenomenon, too, fits the model.[4]

To the degree that major factors such as race and the social class of one's family determined how an actor played the game, it is impossible to conclude that the game was very fair or much of a game at all.

8

An Additional Policy Note

The original intent of this research was to create a body of sociological facts which would be available for public debates on amnesty, should policy makers ever again turn their attention to the subject. At this time, however, this material may be more useful in more pressing policy debates. Some observers of the armed forces are dissatisfied with the progress of the all-volunteer force. Many are calling for the return of conscription or the institution of some form of national service. As the nation makes this or some other future policy alterations, it will always prove wise to reexamine the factual materials which remain part of the legacy of the Second Indochina War.

While there is a considerable body of scholarly work on military service in World War II, there is a dearth of published information on the American servicemen who participated in the Korean Conflict. The actual conditions of service are lost in descriptions of strategic and tactical considerations. Eclipsed by the actions of statesmen and generals, the experience of the ordinary serviceman has given way to the "illusions of the epoch."[1]

General Mark Clark complained after Korea that one of the American military's greatest problems in facing world communism was a deficit of manpower. He felt many of the tasks which had been done by able-bodied GIs in Korea could have been done as well by the handicapped and women. Not until 1959, he predicted, would the United States have available a supply of young men suitable for the necessary confrontation with the vast human resources of the communist forces.[2]

When that expected confrontation with communism finally came about in Indochina, its limited nature combined with the achievements in automation of defense technology did not dictate the tapping of that total pool of available American youth. Instead, the nation was faced with the question: who should serve when not all serve?[3] No single policy maker held the responsibility for this decision. "The best and the brightest" had de-

94

vised the mission.[4] The Selective Service bureaucracy would be relied on
to provide the personnel.

To say that those who composed the first wave of the American expedi-
tionary force to Indochina were all dragged there against their wills would
be misleading. A cult of masculinity nurtured by decades of movies and
centuries of literature provided the necessary core. For the more well-read
among them, war was a rare historical moment; for the rest, a crucible in
which manhood is made.[5] The career military, with pride in its heritage
if not in its pay, stood ready to train, to lead, and to carry out the profession of arms.[6]

The analyses in earlier chapters have shown that belief in the national
purpose reflected in a man's attitude toward the war was indeed an ever
present factor in who served on active duty and who served in Indochina.
Not only those who believed but the nation's finest young men were the
recruits that the career military men wanted to complete their mission in
Southeast Asia. To complete their mission as efficiently and speedily as
possible, they would have indeed needed a special kind of young man.

Two impediments stood in the way of the wants and needs of the military establishment. First, the mission of nation-building and winning the
hearts and minds of the Indochinese people was not very easily translated
into a good operations plan. Second, the supply of talented and fit young
men who were eager to perform such a mission was limited from the outset.

Conscription could be counted on to secure some personnel, and mod-
ernized recruitment techniques coupled with fear of the draft could do the
rest. The patriots and the would-be heroes in search of manhood were joined
in the ranks by men who lived on the outskirts of the Great Society. Minority group members, especially blacks, were a major component of the
ground force, so important for the orchestrated warfare of American foreign policy. At the same time, newly risen black leaders were calling the
war racist and exhorting a generation of black males to a new kind of manhood, manifested by ethnic pride and resistance.

Just as the long-term futility of the American mission was beginning
to seem a reality, a new element was added to the social situation, as men
who had lived outside the mainstream of civilian society were incorporated
into the armed forces by Project 100,000 and other programs. The outraged
editorial policy of the *Army Times* signaled the professionals' welcome for
these men, who epitomized what sociologist Roger Little had called the
combat "dud" in his study of the front line in Korea.[7]

The stage was set not for an assault on the hearts and minds of the people
of Indochina; instead, it was the men of the United States Armed Forces

at every rank whose hearts and minds were under the greatest threat. Machines could destroy Indochinese lives and amass body counts, but machines of destruction were weak in diplomatic skills. The most confusing aspect for the men who thought of themselves as part of the military institution was that in the traditional sense of physically crushing an enemy people, they were winning.

Absence offenses and desertion were only symptomatic of what was slowly happening to the armed forces in Indochina. If desertion were only a social problem to be institutionally solved so that the military could work more efficiently in future Indochinas, the policy suggestions of this book would be simple. They would read as follows:

1. Don't send men into a combat zone until they have had more time in service. The comparison of men who deserted while assigned to Indochina with men who finished their tours only to desert after leaving the combat zone demonstrates this. From previous research, much of it commissioned by the military, it is clear that the social integration of a military unit is the most vital dimension of combat survival and the best available measure against desertion. The primary group level of face to face mutually caring interaction is the key to human sacrifice. Rotation on a yearly basis as it was done in Vietnam creates an atmosphere appropriately reminiscent of factory work minus the potential for camaraderie which goes with being on the same shift.

2. Don't require economically disenfranchised minorities to fight wars for more affluent majorities. It is impossible to deny the role of race in the phenomenon of Vietnam desertion. A greater proportion of black Americans served, and an even greater proportion of black Americans went AWOL.

3. Don't use the "mentally unfit" to provide vital political service for the nation. That men with educational experience well below the national average are overrepresented among deserters is undeniable. If the defense threat is so great, it seems an insane policy to entrust a nation's protection to men who have already been declared institutionally incapable of competing fairly on the labor market. Project 100,000 did just this.

4. Don't use the very young to fight wars. Many post-Vietnam deserters enlisted at a very young age. Given that attitude had much to do with service in the Second Indochina War, this is understandable. Armed conflict, however, remains a stressful situation. Judgment and maturity can be invaluable in coping with stress. Both are frequently associated with age.

5. Don't humiliate military personnel who return from wars. Much of the harassment associated with stateside military service has as its purpose

the creation of the discipline necessary for functioning in combat. Unlike the personnel in previous wars, many Indochina veterans were returned to the context of this petty harassment. This is irrational, and the desertion statistics show that it is dysfunctional.

6. Don't let active duty military personnel be economically deprived. During the Second Indochina War, civilians benefited from a relative economic boom, while military personnel suffered at the market place. A recurrent theme in stated motivations for desertion are crises at home or social instability associated with economic or separation problems. Poor people very often could not afford the luxury of performing military service. Married men at the bottom of the social ladder could especially not afford to do military service.

7. Don't engage in wars of long duration which don't make any sense. In almost every analysis in the preceding chapters, time played an important part. The Second Indochina War was for its participants a dynamic process. As it wore on, the problems associated with it grew. The demoralization of military personnel mirrors the demoralization of the populace. The attitudes of respondents and the attitudes of parents were influential elements in the phenomena statistically analyzed in this book. For this reason, the cognitive processes of the war's participants were crucial, and to them the war just didn't make any sense. A simple exercise in nation-building turned into a defense of honor and a quest for the return of prisoners of war. Service personnel were asked by the people to explain the war, when they should have been the ones asking that question.

Appendix

Statistical Tables and Figures

In order to present the results of a large number of bivariate relationships, this appendix has relied almost totally on correlation coefficients. Correlation coefficients are very good for this, since their values run from positive one $(+1.0)$ to negative one (-1.0). Their meaning can be easily understood, if the reader can grasp the notion of establishing a negative and positive polarity for each variable and then relating that polarity to the changing values of another variable from individual to individual. For example, if education is thought of as years of education and if the length of time that a GI is absent without leave is measured by the time in months that he was AWOL, then it might be stated that education and length of AWOL are positively related, negatively related, or not related at all to any "significant" degree. If these two variables are positively related for any given set of individuals, this would imply that more highly educated military personnel were more likely to report or to have had reported longer periods of AWOL while the less well-educated would be more likely to have shorter reported times AWOL. On the other hand, a negative relationship between education and length of AWOL would imply that, on the average, individuals with greater years of reported education would be more likely to have shorter reported lengths of AWOL, while those with lower levels of education would be more likely to have longer periods of AWOL. It is important to remember than significant levels of association, whether positive or negative, do not imply causality. To say that there is no significant level of association between two variables implies that there is no perceivable relationship between the variables for the data set under consideration.

Here significance is used to refer to the probability that a correlation coefficient is different from zero, which, if it were the case, would mean there existed no relationship between two variables. A .05 level of statistical significance as used here means that there are five chances in one hundred of there *not* being a relationship between two variables.

The following tables are ordered according to the order of the discussions which they support in the text. Relationships between two variables which are dichotomous (have only two possible values such as "yes" and "no") are represented by the phi statistic ($\varnothing$). All other relationships are measured by Pearson product-moment coefficients (r). There is a continuing debate in the social sciences as to whether Pearson's zero-order correlation coefficients which are calculated from rank-order level data are an acceptable measure of association. (See Robert M. O'Brien, "Using Rank-Order Measures to Represent Continuous Variables," *Social Forces* 61 (September 1982): 144–155, for the most recent sociological input on this debate.) Since this debate remains unresolved — and will continue in this status for some time — the levels of significance reported for rank-order variables should be considered with appropriate caution.

The only rank-order variable utilized in this research is social class (sometimes designated SES in the tables). No levels of significance are presented for this variable in any of the tables, though this variable is included as a minor element in some of the regression computations. Regression, however, is a stronger test of a rank-order variable's usefulness. Above all, it must be noted that doubt concerning the utility of this particular measure of social class has already been presented in the text.

Chapter Three

The variables on AWOL, times AWOL, and length of longest AWOL are abstracted from the following survey items.

Label	Survey Question
AWOL	A lot of soldiers went AWOL in the military. Did you ever go AWOL — even for a short period of time?
Times AWOL	How many times did you go AWOL? (1) Once (2) Twice (3) Three or more times

(Answer only if you ever went AWOL): What was the longest you were ever AWOL?
(1) Less than 24 hours.
(2) More than 24 hours, but less than three days.
(3) Three days or more, but less than a month.
(4) A month or more, but less than a year.
(5) A year or more.

Table 3-1.   Correlation Coefficients between AWOL Variables and
Social Background Items for Notre Dame Survey (NDS)

	AWOL	Times AWOL
Age	− .126**	− .090*
	(518)	(518)
White	− .198***	− .197***
	(524)	(524)
Education	− .243***	− .192***
	(525)	(525)
Social class of family	− .171***	− .148***
	(519)	(519)
Two parents in home	− .121**	− .053
	(524)	(524)
Father veteran	.040	.011
	(516)	(516)
Parents opposed draft	.002	.038
	(519)	(519)
Respondent favored war	− .016	− .041
	(524)	(524)
Respondent avoided draft	− .092*	− .061
	(463)	(463)

*Significant at .05 level.

**Significant at .01 level.

***Significant at .001 level.

Table 3-3.   Correlation Coefficients between AWOL Variables
and Military Career Variables (NDS)

	AWOL	Times AWOL
Drafted	.162***	.164***
	(524)	(524)
Ground Force (Army or Marines)	− .057	− .050
	(525)	(525)
Time in Service	.022	− .017
	(521)	(521)
Personnel manipulation attempts	− .023	.002
	(480)	(480)
Vietnam service	.151***	.138***
	(509)	(509)
Combat service	.158**	.127*
	(221)	(221)

*Significant at .05 level.

**Significant at .01 level.

***Significant at .001 level.

Table 3-4.　Correlation Coefficients between AWOL Length
and Social Background Variables (NDS)

	AWOL Length		AWOL Length
Age	− .162 (143)	Education	− .083 (146)
White	.026 (146)	Social class	.063 (143)
Both natural parents in home	− .081 (146)	Favored war	− .139* (145)
Veteran father	.011 (141)	Attempted to avoid draft	.100 (137)
Parents opposed draft	.036 (143)		

*Significant at .05 level.

Table 3-5.　Correlation Coefficients between AWOL Length
and Social Background Variables (PCB)

	AWOL Length		AWOL Length
Age	− .182*** (1004)	Two types of family instability	.078** (1008)
White	− .074** (992)	Evidence of economic instability	.112*** (1008)
Both natural parents in home	− .065* (763)	Number of siblings	.006 (880)
Urban/suburban origin	− .033 (326)	Years of education	.035 (953)
Southern origin	− .010 (787)	Unmarried	− .139*** (766)
One type of family instability	.071** (1008)		

*Significant at .05 level.

**Significant at .01 level.

***Significant at .001 level.

Table 3-6.   **Correlation Coefficients between AWOL Length**
                        and Military Career Variables (NDS)

	AWOL Length		AWOL Length
Drafted	.009	Combat Service	.143
	(146)		(82)
Ground force	.013	Times AWOL	.154*
	(146)		(141)
Time in service	−.112	Legally postponed	.204**
	(145)	active duty	(137)
Vietnam service	.093	Number personnel	.216**
	(144)	manipulation attempts	(135)

*Significant at .05 level.

**Significant at .01 level.

Table 3-7.   **Correlation Coefficients between AWOL Length**
                        and Military Career Variables (PCB)

	AWOL Length		AWOL Length
Drafted	.184***	Vietnam service	−.023
	(788)		(1008)
AFQT category	.055*	Voluntary surrender	−.025
	(911)		(699)
Age at induction	.221***	Employed while AWOL	.180**
	(999)		(213)
Time in service	−.027	Times AWOL	−.135***
	(992)		(1008)

*Significant at .05 level.

**Significant at .01 level.

***Significant at .001 level.

The survey question on which the variable labeled Punishment is based, is as follows:

(Answer only if you ever went AWOL): How were you punished for your longest AWOL?
(1) I was never punished for it.
(2) I only lost a few privileges.
(3) I was fined, lost rank, or confined to quarters — but not by a court-martial.
(4) I was court-martialed.

Table 3-8.   Correlation Coefficients between Punishment
                  and Background Variables (NDS)

	Punishment		Punishment
Age	−.218***	Drafted	.127*
	(144)		(147)
White	.075	Ground force	.032
	(147)		(147)
Both natural parents in home	−.012	Time in service	−.135**
	(147)		(146)
Father veteran	.085	Vietnam service	.096
	(143)		(144)
Parents opposed draft	−.063	Combat service	.157*
	(143)		(83)
Attempted to avoid draft	.151**	NDS AWOL length	.517****
	(139)		(145)
Education	−.171**	Times AWOL	.045
	(147)		(141)
Social class	.070	Personnel manipulations	.064
	(143)		(135)
Favored war	−.117*		
	(146)		

*Significant at .10 level.

**Significant at .05 level.

***Significant at .01 level.

****Significant at .001 level.

Table 3-9.   **Correlation Coefficients between Military Justice
                        Variables and Social Background Variables (NDS)**

	Months Sentenced	Months Confined
Age	− .213***	− .186***
	(1004)	(1004)
White	.029	.068*
	(992)	(992)
Both natural parents in home	− .047	− .031
	(763)	(763)
Urban/suburban	− .130**	− .052
	(326)	(326)
Southern	.057*	.028
	(787)	(787)
One type family instability	.150***	.151***
	(1008)	(1008)
Two types family instability	.169***	.171***
	(1008)	(1008)
Economic instability	.170***	.166***
	(1008)	(1008)
Number of siblings	.077**	.074**
	(880)	(880)
Years of education	− .049	− .068*
	(953)	(953)
Single	− .054	− .038
	(766)	(766)

*Significant at .05 level.

**Significant at .01 level.

***Significant at .001 level.

Table 3-10.   **Correlation Coefficients between Military Justice Variables and Military Career and Offense-Related Variables (NDS)**

	Months Sentenced	Months Confined
Drafted	.080**	.072*
	(788)	(788)
Army	−.087**	−.113***
	(1008)	(1008)
Marine Corps	.067*	.074**
	(1008)	(1008)
Age of enlistment	.057*	.025
	(999)	(999)
Time in service	−.098***	−.092**
	(992)	(992)
Previous request for hardship discharge	.049	.063*
	(1008)	(1008)
Voluntary surrender	−.098**	−.094**
	(699)	(699)
Not in hiding	−.089*	−.083*
	(397)	(397)
Employed while AWOL	−.019	−.043
	(213)	(213)
Times AWOL	.029	.031
	(1008)	(1008)
PCB AWOL length	.175***	.132***
	(1008)	(1008)
Physical/psychological problems	.076**	.072**
	(1007)	(1007)

*Significant at .05 level.

**Significant at .01 level.

***Significant at .001 level.

Chapter Four

Table 4-3.   **Two Groups of Deserters by Race (PCB)**

	White	Non-White	Data Missing	Totals
Deserters from in-country assignments	36 (61.0%)	23 (39.0%)	0	59
Post-Vietnam deserters	143 (73.7%)	51 (26.3%)	4	198
Totals	179	74	4	257

Table 4-4.   **Two Groups of Deserters by Presence Two Parents in Home of Origin (PCB)**

	Two-Parent Homes	Non-Two-Parent Homes	Data Missing	Totals
Deserters from in-country assignments	18 (41.9%)	25 (58.1%)	16	59
Post-Vietnam deserters	76 (52.8%)	68 (47.2%)	54	198
Totals	94	93	70	257

Table 4-5.   **Two Groups of Deserters by Evidence of Family Instability (PCB)**

	Evidence of Instability	No Evidence of Instability	Totals
Deserters from in-country assignments	22 (37.3%)	37 (62.7%)	59
Post-Vietnam deserters	51 (25.8%)	147 (74.2%)	198
Totals	73	184	257

Table 4-6.   **Two Groups of Deserters by Type of Military Intake (PCB)**

	Drafted	Enlisted	Data Missing	Totals
Deserters from in-country assignments	11 (19.6%)	45 (80.4%)	3	59
Post-Vietnam deserters	13 (6.6%)	183 (93.4%)	2	198
Totals	24	228	5	257

Table 4-7. **Two Groups of Deserters by Time in Service (PCB)**

	Less than 12 mos.	13–24 mos.	25–36 mos.	Over 3 yrs.	Totals
Deserters from in-country assignments	11	30	10	8	59
Post-Vietnam deserters	7	48	75	68	198
Totals	18	78	85	76	257

Table 4-8. **Two Groups of Deserters by Evidence of Hardship Personnel Actions (PCB)**

	No Evidence of Requests	Granted Requests	Denied Requests	Data Missing	Totals
Deserters from in-country assignments	56 (94.9%)	1 (1.7%)	2 (3.4%)	0	59
Post-Vietnam deserters	168 (85.5%)	5 (2.5%)	24 (12.2%)	1	198
Totals	224	6	26	1	257

Table 4-9. **Two Groups of Deserters by Type of Vietnam Duty (PCB)**

	Non-Combat Duty	Combat Duty	No Distinction Made	Totals
Deserters from in-country assignments	11 (42.3%)	15 (57.7%)	33	59
Post-Vietnam deserters	23 (21.1%)	86 (78.9%)	89	198
Totals	34	101	122	257

Chapter Five

Table 5-1. **Education Levels of Jehovah's Witnesses (PCB)**

	N	Percent
Less than high school diploma	16	19.2
High school diploma	52	62.7
Some college or grade school	11	13.2
Information not available	10	

Table 5-2.   **Occupation at Time of Presidential Clemency Board**
                       Hearings for Jehovah's Witnesses in Sample

	N	Percent
White collar, full time	10	20.4
Skilled blue collar, full time	12	24.5
Unskilled blue collar, full time	14	28.6
White collar, part time	1	2.0
Unskilled blue collar, part time	3	6.1
Intermittently employed	3	6.1
College student	2	4.1
Incarcerated	4	8.2
Information not available	44	

Table 5-3.   **Percentage of Jehovah's Witnesses for which**
                       PCB Background Problem Categories Apply

One-Parent Home	Family Instability	Economic Instability	Personal Problems Related to Offense
32.4	26.8	20.4	3.2

Table 5-4.   **Marital Status of Jehovah's Witnesses (PCB)**

	N	Percent
Single	21	26.3
Divorced/separated	2	2.5
Married, no children	31	28.7
Married, children	26	32.5

Table 5-5.   **Racial Background of Jehovah's Witnesses (PCB)**

	N	Percent
White	80	86.0
Black	10	10.6
Spanish surname	2	2.1
Other	1	1.1

Table 5-6.   **Conditions of Arrest and Trial for Jehovah's Witnesses (PCB)**

	Voluntary Surrender		In Hiding		Guilty Plea	
	N	Percent	N	Percent	N	Percent
Yes	37	86.0	1	2.9	46	82.1
No	6	14.0	33	97.1	10	17.9
No information	50		59		37	

Table 5-7.   **Sentences, Incarceration, and Probation for Jehovah's Witnesses (PCB)**

Months	Sentenced		Served		Probation	
	N	Percent	N	Percent	N	Percent
None	22	23.7	74	79.6	18	19.4
1–12	4	4.3	6	6.4	9	9.7
13–24	11	11.8	11	11.8	15	16.1
25–36	19	20.4	0	0.0	37	39.8
37–48	8	8.6	2	2.2	5	5.4
49–60	22	23.7	0	0.0	9	9.7
Over 60	7	7.5	0	0.0	0	0.0

Table 5-8.   **Correlation Coefficients between "Jehovah's Witness" and Selected Variables (PCB)**

Years of education	−.141***	White	−.068
	(444)		(392)
White collar	−.063	Surrendered	.157**
	(277)		(277)
Two parent home	−.097*	Plea of guilty	−.001
	(394)		(234)
Family instability	−.046	Incarceration	.033
	(468)	(months sentenced)	(468)
Economic instability	−.082*	Incarceration	−.020
	(468)	(months served)	(468)
Personal problems	−.147***	Months on probation	.044
	(468)		(468)
Married	.238***		
	(370)		

*Significant at the .05 level of significance.

**Significant at the .01 level of significance.

***Significant at the .001 level of significance.

Table 5-9.   **Varieties of Vietnam Service among**
                       Military Absence Offenders (PCB)

	N	Percent
Partial tour ending in injury	15	1.4
Full tour	165	16.4
More than one tour	30	3.0
Completed Vietnam service	210	20.8
Partial tour ending administratively	34	3.4
Partial tour ending in AWOL	24	2.4
No Vietnam tour	741	73.4
	1,009	100.0

Table 5-10.   **Correlation Coefficients between "Vietnam service"**
                       and Chronological Variables (PCB)

Year of birth	− .123***	Time in service	.498***
	(1004)		(992)
Year of offense	.112***	Year left active duty	.077**
	(973)		(991)
Age at enlistment	− .096***		
	(999)		

  **Significant at .01 level.

***Significant at .001 level.

Table 5-11.   **Correlation Coefficients between "Vietnam service"**
                       and Social Background Variables (PCB)

White	− .001	AFQT category	− .072*
	(992)		(911)
Years of education	.061*	Family instability	− .083**
	(953)		(1008)
Southern origin	− .066*	Economic instability	− .056*
	(787)		(1008)
Married	− .055	Personal problems	.107***
	(766)		(1007)
IQ	.092**		
	(884)		

 *Significant at .05 level.

 **Significant at .01 level.

***Significant at .001 level.

Table 5-12.   **Physical or Psychological Problems Related to Offense
                   for Cases with Completed Vietnam Service (PCB)**

	N	Percent
Physical problems	16	7.6
Psychological problems	46	21.9
Drug problems	13	6.2
Alcohol problems	4	1.9
None	131	62.4

Table 5-13.   **Mode of Induction for Military Absence Offenders
                   with Completed Vietnam Tours (PCB)**

	N	Percent
Drafted	15	7.1
Two year enlistment	17	8.1
Three year enlistment	101	48.1
Reenlisted	39	18.6
Enlisted (length unspecified)	34	16.2
Judicially induced enlistment	1	0.5
Information unavailable	3	1.4

Table 5-14.   **Correlation Coefficients between Variables Relating to
                   Conditions of Absence Offenses and "Vietnam service" (PCB)**

AWOLS (unpunished)	.096*** (1008)	Total AWOLS	.139*** (1008)
AWOLS (nonjudicial punishment)	.172*** (1008)	Surrendered	− .004 (649)
AWOLS (summary court martial)	.026 (1008)	In hiding	− .025 (397)
AWOLS (special court martial)	− .041 (1008)	Total months AWOL	− .023 (1008)
AWOLS (general court martial)	− .076** (1008)		

**Significant at .01 level.

***Significant at .001 level.

Table 5-15.   **Sentences and Length of Incarceration for Military Absence Offenders with Completed Vietnam Tour (PCB)**

| | Sentenced | | Incarcerated | |
	N	Percent	N	Percent
None	145	69.0	132	62.9
1–6 months	47	22.4	67	31.9
7–12 months	16	7.6	11	5.2
Over 12 months	2	1.0	0	0.0

Table 5-16.   **Ethnicity among Project 100,000 Personnel (PCB)**

	N	Percent
Caucasian	163	55.4
Black	108	36.7
Native American	3	1.0
Spanish surname	18	6.1
Race not identified	2	0.7

Table 5-17.   **Correlation Coefficients between Project 100,000 Membership and Selected Background Variables (PCB)**

White	$-.299$***	Unstable family	$-.066$*
	(910)		(922)
Year of birth	$-.012$	Economic deprivation	.059*
	(919)		(922)
Southern	.140***	Years of education	$-.217$***
	(718)		(869)
Both natural parents	$-.090$**		
	(695)		

  *Significant at .05 level.

 **Significant at .01 level.

***Significant at .001 level.

Table 5-18.   **Mode of Induction to Active Duty for Project 100,000 Personnel (PCB)**

	N	Percent
Drafted	74	32.2
Enlisted	154	67.0
Judicially induced enlistment	2	0.8
No information	64	

Table 5-19. **Correlation Coefficients between Project 100,000 Membership and Selected Military Service and Incidents of Offense Variables (PCB)**

Drafted	.210***	Times AWOL	− .042
	(715)		(911)
Age of induction	.137***	Months AWOL	.100***
	(911)		(922)
Vietnam service	− .038	Voluntary surrender	.050
	(922)		(632)
Time in service	− .135***	In hiding	.060
	(908)		(361)
Army	.214***	Months sentenced	.012
	(922)		(911)
Marines	− .129***	Months incarcerated	− .039
	(922)		(911)

***Significant at .001 level.

Table 5-20. **Civilian Criminal Records of Military Absence Offenders (PCB)**

	N	Percent
Multiple violent felonies	7	0.7
Nonviolent and violent felonies	13	1.3
Violent felony	32	3.2
Nonviolent felony	64	6.3
No civilian crimes	893	88.5

Table 5-21. **Non-Absence Offenses of Military Absence Offenders (PCB)**

	N	Percent
General court martial offense	8	0.8
Special court martial offense	312	30.9
Summary court martial offense	74	7.3
Non-judicial punishment offense	174	17.2
Undesirable for military (nonpunishable assessment)	13	1.3
No non-absence offenses	428	42.4

Table 5-22.   **Non-Absence Offenses Which Would Have Been**
                       Civilian Crimes for Military Absence Offenders (PCB)

	N	Percent
General court martial offense	2	0.2
Special court martial offense	16	1.6
Summary court martial offense	6	0.6
Non-judicial punishment offense	5	0.5
No military offense which would have been a civilian crime	980	97.1

Table 5-23.   **Correlation Coefficients between Two types of Criminal**
                       Records and Selected Social Background Variables (PCB)

	Civilian Crimes	Non-Absence Military Crimes
White	− .093**	− .027
	(991)	(979)
Year of birth	.056*	− .139**
	(1003)	(991)
Southern	.058*	.045
	(787)	(777)
Both natural parents	− .079*	− .008
	(762)	(753)
Family instability	.063*	.049
	(1007)	(995)
Economic deprivation	− .053*	.025
	(1007)	(995)
Years of education	− .058*	− .048
	(952)	(941)
Full time employment	− .155**	.050
	(213)	(213)

*Significant at .05 level.

**Significant at .01 level.

Table 5-24.   **Correlation Coefficients for Types of Criminal Record,**
                       Vietnam Service, and Project 100,000 Membership (PCB)

	Civilian Crimes	Non-Absence Military Crimes
Vietnam service	− .012	.001
	(1007)	(995)
Project 100,000	.032	− .003
	(922)	(912)

Table 5-25.   **Correlation Coefficients between Two Types of Criminal Record and Military Service and Absence Offense Variables (PCB)**

	Civilian Crimes	Non-Absence Military Crimes
Drafted	− .041	− .012
	(787)	(778)
Age at induction	− .056*	− .081**
	(998)	(986)
Time in service	− .044	.127***
	(991)	(979)
Army	− .002	− .122***
	(1007)	(995)
Marines	− .006	.082**
	(1007)	(995)
Application for hardship discharge	− .054*	.062*
	(1007)	(995)
Times AWOL	.017	.315***
	(1007)	(995)
Months AWOL	− .071**	− .047
	(1007)	(995)
Surrender	− .023	− .082*
	(699)	(693)
In hiding	− .080	.070
	(396)	(392)

*Significant at .05 level.

**Significant at .01 level.

***Significant at .001 level.

Table 5-26.   **Blacks and Draftees as Percent of Armed Forces Assigned to Vietnam and as Percent of Combat Deaths**

	Blacks as Percent of Vietnam Force	Blacks as Percent of Casualties	Draftees as Percent of Vietnam Force	Draftees as Percent of Casualties
1965	12.0	14.6	14.7	Not Available
1966	10.6	16.0	29.3	21
1967	9.8	14.1	28.9	34
1968	10.9	13.5	30.2	34
1969	9.7	12.9	24.9	40
1970	11.5	12.5	23.7	43
1971	9.5	12.4	19.4	33
1972	8.7	12.3	4.3	6
1973	Less than .05	12.3	5.2	4

Source: Statistical Abstract of the U.S. (1970, 1974).

Chapter Six

Table 6-2.   Correlation Coefficients between Draft Avoidance Behaviors (NDS)

	(2)	(3)	(4)	(5)	(6)	(7)	(8)	(9)	(10)	(11)	(12)
(1) Late registration	.047* (1544)	.026 (1551)	-.093 (1541)	.002 (1526)	-.008 (1554)	.003 (1554)	.014 (1455)	-.020 (1515)	.015 (1492)	-.019 (1513)	.029 (1488)
(2) Learning		.500*** (1548)	.305*** (1539)	.178*** (1522)	.075*** (1551)	.027 (1552)	.188*** (1451)	.329*** (1512)	.1781*** (1488)	.1806*** (1510)	.1596*** (1485)
(3) Expert counseling			.291*** (1548)	.167*** (1532)	.089*** (1558)	.027 (1560)	.183*** (1459)	.347*** (1520)	.164*** (1497)	.160*** (1517)	.160*** (1491)
(4) Application				.171*** (1522)	.048* (1549)	.023 (1551)	.147*** (1453)	.306*** (1511)	.133*** (1488)	.115*** (1509)	.128*** (1484)
(5) School					.148*** (1532)	.077*** (1534)	.210*** (1445)	.143*** (1504)	.097*** (1483)	.108*** (1495)	.097*** (1470)
(6) Marriage						.435*** (1563)	.149*** (1461)	.043* (1521)	.014 (1498)	.026 (1519)	-.023 (1493)
(7) Children							.108*** (1463)	.012 (1523)	.013 (1500)	.000 (1520)	-.016 (1494)
(8) Career								.139*** (1457)	.088 (1432)	.230*** (1428)	.181*** (1404)
(9) Doctor									.304 (1493)	.153*** (1488)	.126*** (1462)
(10) Mutilate										.193*** (1468)	.110*** (1448)
(11) Other											.237*** (1485)
(12) More											

*Significant at .05 level.

**Significant at .01 level.

***Significant at .001 level.

Table 6-3.   **Correlation Coefficients between Draft Avoidance Behaviors and Military Service (NDS)**

	Serve		Serve
Late registration	.020	Career	− .013
	(1550)		(1457)
Learning	− .238***	Doctor	− .171***
	(1547)		(1518)
Expert Counseling	− .160***	Mutilate	− .087***
	(1555)		(1495)
Application	− .254***	Other	− .025
	(1546)		(1515)
School	.022	More	.004
	(1530)		(1491)
Marriage	.024	Resist	− .155***
	(1557)		(1341)
Children	− .004		
	(1559)		

***Significant at .001 level.

Table 6-4.   **Confirmatory Factor Analysis of Ten Avoidance Strategies (n = 1437) (NDS)**

	Factor 1	Factor 2	Factor 3	Factor 4
Late registration	.025	.007	.912*	.254
Learning	.714*	− .153	− .153	− .066
Expert counseling	.706*	− .145	.099	− .068
Application	.580*	− .158	− .286	− .183
School	.448	.197	.163	− .396
Marriage	.267	.778*	− .074	.103
Children	.184	.779*	− .100	.267
Career	.443	.209	.165	− .355
Doctor	.640	− .238	− .186	− .281
Mutilate	.419	− .182	− .061	.654*

Table 6-5. **Correlation Coefficients between each Draft Avoidance Behavior and Background Variables (NDS)**

	White	Both Natural Parents in Home	Father Served in Military	Parents Oppposed Draft	SES	Respondent Favored Vietnam War
Late registration	−.171***	−.172***	−.074**	−.018	−.167	−.043
	(1550)[a]	(1550)	(1544)	(1550)	(1543)	(1552)
Learning	.004	.028	.018	.298***	.096	−.142***
	(1547)	(1548)	(1541)	(1545)	(1539)	(1549)
Expert counseling	.057**	.003	.063**	.219***	.115	−.134***
	(1555)	(1555)	(1549)	(1553)	(1547)	(1557)
Application	.126***	.049*	.017	.161***	.127	−.135***
	(1545)	(1546)	(1539)	(1543)	(1537)	(1547)
School	.094***	.005	.008	.075**	.048	−.057**
	(1529)	(1529)	(1523)	(1528)	(1524)	(1531)
Marriage	−.039	−.055*	−.021	−.019	−.053	−.054*
	(1557)	(1557)	(1551)	(1555)	(1549)	(1559)
Children	.005	−.033	−.003	.007	.004	−.009
	(1559)	(1559)	(1553)	(1557)	(1551)	(1561)
Career	.053*	.027	−.025	.037	.031	−.058
	(1457)	(1458)	(1452)	(1455)	(1451)	(1459)
Doctor	.099***	.034	.016	.205***	.103	−.101***
	(1518)	(1519)	(1512)	(1516)	(1512)	(1520)
Mutilate	.027	.045*	.025	.143***	.030	−.041
	(1495)	(1495)	(1489)	(1493)	(1490)	(1497)
Other	.067**	.034	.017	.030	.041	.001
	(1516)	(1516)	(1509)	(1513)	(1509)	(1517)
More	.104***	.069**	.013	.068**	.057	−.057*
	(1490)	(1490)	(1484)	(1487)	(1483)	(1491)
Total avoidance	.087***	−.003	−.017	.233***	.091	−.153***
behavior	(1338)	(1338)	(1333)	(1337)	(1334)	(1339)

*Significant at .05 level of significance.

**Significant at .01 level of significance.

***Significant at .001 level of significance.

[a]Number of cases in each computation is in parentheses below coefficient.

Table 6-6.　　　　　　Correlation Coefficients between Social Demographic
　　　　　　　　　　　Variables and Draft Avoidance Behavior (NDS)

	Age	Education
Late registration	−.038	−.156***
	(1537)	(1556)
Learning	−.161***	.148***
	(1536)	(1553)
Expert counseling	−.079***	.144***
	(1542)	(1561)
Application	.045*	.331***
	(1532)	(1551)
School	.079***	.100***
	(1517)	(1535)
Marriage	.058***	−.010
	(1544)	(1563)
Children	.047*	−.018
	(1546)	(1565)
Career	.068**	.129***
	(1444)	(1463)
Doctor	−.028	.120***
	(1506)	(1524)
Mutilate	−.005	.033
	(1483)	(1501)
Other	.034	.063**
	(1502)	(1521)
More	.017	.110***
	(1478)	(1495)
Resist 1	.040	.219***
	(1329)	(1343)
Resist 2	−.076**	.260***
	(1435)	(1435)

*Significant at .05 level of significance.

**Significant at .01 level of significance.

***Significant at .001 level of significance.

Table 6-7.   Correlation Coefficients between Draft Classifications and Selected Variables (NDS)

	Military Service	Age	White	Parents Opposed Draft	Avoided Draft	Education	Social Class	Respondent Favored War
Available for service (1-A)	.245*** (1444)	.155*** (1432)	-.013 (1445)	-.041 (1444)	-.019 (1369)	-.074** (1450)	-.051 (1437)	.051* (1447)
Student deferment	-.233*** (1491)	-.013 (1470)	.209*** (1491)	.174*** (1489)	.325*** (1415)	.542*** (1497)	.260 (1483)	-.117*** (1494)
Graduate deferment	-.114*** (1485)	.140*** (1473)	.059* (1484)	.075** (1483)	.155*** (1411)	.283*** (1490)	.097 (1489)	-.061** (1486)
Hardship deferment	-.120*** (1497)	.162*** (1485)	-.038 (1497)	.020 (1495)	.020 (1423)	-.044* (1503)	-.097 (1489)	-.007 (1499)
Occupational deferment	-.099*** (1499)	.119*** (1486)	.011 (1499)	-.008 (1497)	.058* (1425)	.112*** (1505)	.027 (1491)	-.048* (1501)
Physical exemption	-.242*** (1497)	.070** (1485)	.071** (1497)	.076** (1495)	.060** (1422)	.028 (1503)	.016 (1489)	-.024 (1499)
Psychological or mental exemption	-.086*** (1502)	.044* (1490)	-.015 (1502)	.024 (1500)	.045* (1428)	-.079*** (1508)	-.059 (1494)	-.018 (1504)
Conscientious objector	-.097*** (1495)	-.021 (1483)	.015 (1495)	.032 (1493)	.089*** (1422)	.009 (1501)	.028 (1487)	-.033 (1497)

*Significant at the .05 level of significance.

**Significant at the .01 level of significance.

***Significant at the .001 level of significance.

Table 6-8.   **Correlation Coefficients between Having a High Lottery Number and Selected Variables (NDS)**

	High Number		High Number
Military service	− .356***	Father served in military	.101***
	(1558)		(1552)
Age	− .402***	Social class	.188
	(1545)		(1550)
White	.079***	Respondent favored war	− .153***
	(1558)		(1560)
Parents present in home	.100***	Education	.143***
	(1558)		(1564)
Student deferment	.119***		
	(1495)		

***Significant at the .001 level of significance.

Table 6-9.   **Correlation Coefficients between Attitudinal Answers (NDS)**

	(2)	(3)	(4)	(5)	(6)
(1) Draft fair	.487***	.047*	.055*	.262***	.189***
	(1358)	(1437)	(1426)	(533)	(1414)
(2) Draft fair		.101***	.101***	.339***	.158***
to friends		(1417)	(1410)	(540)	(1394)
(3) Respondent			.491***	.404***	.018
favored war			(1540)	(577)	(1522)
(4) Now favors war				.504***	.040
				(577)	(1507)
(5) Attitude towards					.164***
government					(572)
(6) Avoid more					

*Significant at .05 level.

**Significant at .01 level.

***Significant at .001 level.

Table 6-10.   Correlation Coefficients between Attitude and Selected Variables (NDS)

	Draft Fair	Draft Fair to Friends	Respondent Favored War	Now Favors War	Attitude Towards Government	Avoid More
Military service	-.027 (1437)	.029 (1414)	.229*** (1556)	.135 (1535)	.111** (578)	-.134*** (1520)
Age	.031 (1425)	.085*** (1402)	.181*** (1543)	.129*** (1522)	.236*** (573)	.073** (1508)
White	.106*** (1436)	.188*** (1414)	.032 (1556)	.042* (1535)	.002 (576)	.022 (1520)
Parents opposed draft	-.060* (1438)	-.096*** (1416)	-.102*** (1554)	-.053* (1534)	-.172** (577)	-.076** (1519)
Attempted to avoid draft	-.133*** (1368)	-.184*** (1343)	-.212*** (1477)	-.207*** (1457)	-.340*** (545)	-.085*** (1445)
Education	.050* (1441)	.005 (1420)	-.147*** (1562)	-.124*** (1541)	-.218*** (579)	.032 (1526)
SES	.044 (1437)	.046 (1410)	-.084 (1548)	-.089 (1529)	-.117 (573)	-.035 (1515)
Actually drafted	-.081*** (1440)	-.015 (1419)	.056** (1561)	.061** (1540)	.030 (579)	-.074** (1525)

*Significant at .05 level of significance.

**Significant at .01 level of significance.

***Significant at .001 level of significance.

Figure 6-11.   **Path Model of Effective Draft Resistance**
and Military Service (NDS)

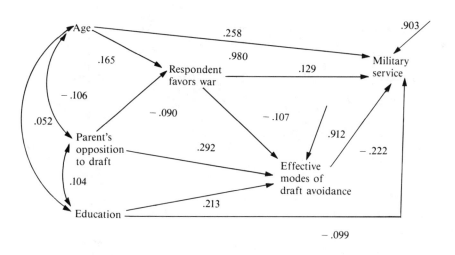

Table 6-12.   **Correlation Matrix for Path Model in Figure 6-11 (NDS)**

	(1)	(2)	(3)	(4)	(5)	(6)
(1) Age	1.000	−.106	.052	.175	−.076	.292
(2) Parents oppose draft		1.000	.104	−.108	.326	−.099
(3) Education			1.000	−.155	.260	−.163
(4) Respondent favors war				1.000	−.171	.227
(5) Effective modes of draft avoidance					1.000	−.290
(6) Military service						1.000

Chapter Seven

Table 7-2. **Correlation Coefficients between Personnel Manipulation Variables (NDS)**

	(2)	(3)	(4)	(5)	(6)	(7)
(1) Postponed service	.221***	.191***	.151***	.133***	.070*	.067
	(514)	(519)	(521)	(522)	(520)	(507)
(2) Enlisted in low-		.488***	.061	.149***	.059	.097**
involvement branch		(540)	(540)	(543)	(541)	(527)
(3) Enlisted in low-			.233***	.276***	.122**	.152***
risk MOS			(546)	(547)	(543)	(530)
(4) Changed to low-				.505***	.163***	.164***
risk MOS				(549)	(546)	(532)
(5) Volunteer long-term					.174***	.200***
low-risk assignment					(548)	(535)
(6) In-service CO						.149***
application						(535)
(7) Other						

*Significant at .05 level.

**Significant at .01 level.

***Significant at .001 level.

Table 7-3. **Confirmatory Factor Analysis of Personnel Structure Manipulation after One Orthagonal Rotation (NDS)**

	Factor 1	Factor 2	Factor 3
Postponed service	.575*	.196	− .078
Enlisted in low-involvement branch	.851*	− .077	.055
Enlisted in low-risk MOS	.773*	.184	.126
Change to low-risk MOS	.064	.873*	.062
Volunteer long-term low-risk assignment	.176	.829*	.093
In-service CO application	.046	.119	.983*

Table 7-4.   Correlation Coefficients between Personnel Manipulation
                    Variables and Vietnam Service, Combat Service (NDS)

	Vietnam Service	Combat Service
Postponed service	$-.121$***	$-.152$**
	(508)	(215)
Enlisted in low-involvement branch	$-.186$***	$-.199$***
	(527)	(226)
Enlisted in low-risk MOS	$-.156$***	$-.180$**
	(529)	(225)
Changed to low-risk MOS	$-.065$	$-.051$
	(532)	(226)
Volunteer long-term low-risk assignment	$-.059$	$-.040$
	(535)	(228)
In-service CO application	$-.018$	$-.168$**
	(534)	(226)
Other	$-.115$**	$-.067$
	(526)	(224)
Personnel manipulation	$-.182$***	$-.218$***
	(494)	(214)

**Significant at .01 level.

***Significant at .001 level.

Table 7-5. Correlation Coefficients between Personnel Manipulation Variables and Background Variables (NDS)

	White	Both Natural Parents in Home	Father Served in Military	Parents Opposed Draft	SES	Respondent Favored Vietnam War	Age	Education
Postponed service	.088* (529)	.044 (529)	.037 (521)	.151*** (525)	.096** (525)	-.118** (529)	-.007 (523)	.124** (530)
Enlisted in low-involvement branch	.069* (546)	.107 (546)	.062 (539)	.176*** (540)	.096** (541)	-.198*** (546)	-.097** (540)	.145*** (547)
Enlisted in low-risk MOS	.049 (549)	.108 (549)	.046 (541)	.107** (543)	.085* (544)	-.157*** (549)	-.090* (543)	.089* (550)
Changed to low-risk MOS	.018 (551)	.028 (549)	.012 (543)	.070* (545)	-.077* (544)	-.099** (549)	-.025 (545)	-.002 (552)
Volunteer long-term low-risk assignment	.011 (554)	.013 (554)	.067 (546)	.033* (548)	-.008 (546)	-.080 (551)	-.094** (548)	-.073* (555)
In-service CO application	.009 (552)	-.019 (552)	.013 (544)	.029 (546)	-.043 (547)	-.084* (554)	-.041 (546)	-.090 (553)
Other	.041 (539)	.015 (539)	.075* (532)	.042 (534)	.038 (536)	-.081* (552)	-.006 (534)	.051 (540)
Personnel manipulation	.065 (507)	.085* (506)	.076* (500)	.167*** (501)	.051 (503)	-.226*** (539)	-.127** (501)	.043 (507)

*Significant at .05 level.

**Significant at .01 level.

***Significant at .001 level.

Table 7-6.   **Correlation Coefficients between Personnel Manipulation Variables and Military Career Variables (NDS)**

	Drafted	Army or Marines	Year Entered	Time in Service
Postponed service	.093*	.043	.176***	−.252***
	(530)	(530)	(530)	(522)
Enlisted in low-involvement branch			−.027	−.103**
			(547)	(543)
Enlisted in low-risk MOS		−.067	−.008	−.030
		(550)	(550)	(546)
Changed to low-risk MOS	.116**	.033	−.011	−.021
	(551)	(552)	(552)	(548)
Volunteer long-term low-risk assignment	.078*	−.038	−.046	.076*
	(554)	(555)	(555)	(551)
In-service CO application	.062	−.017	.044	.007
	(552)	(553)	(553)	(549)
Other	.037	−.030	−.034	−.107**
	(539)	(540)	(540)	(535)
Personnel manipulation	−.034	−.044	−.021	−.063
	(506)	(507)	(507)	(504)

*Significant at .05 level.

**Significant at .01 level.

***Significant at .001 level.

Table 7-7.   **Correlation Coefficients between In-Vietnam Measure to Avoid Combat and Correlation Coefficients between these Measures and Combat Service (NDS)**

	(2)	(3)	(4)	(5)
(1) Saigon	.727***	.194**	.245***	−.093
	(230)	(228)	(224)	(226)
(2) Non-combat job		.311***	.313***	−.094
		(226)	(218)	(223)
(3) Reduce			.126*	−.005
			(215)	(225)
(4) Pre-Vietnam personnel manipulation				−.218***
				(214)
(5) Combat service				

*Significant at .05 level.

**Significant at .01 level.

***Significant at .001 level.

Table 7-8. Correlation Coefficients for 396 Cases on 11 Variables used to Construct Model of Vietnam Service and Personnel Manipulation (NDS)

	(2)	(3)	(4)	(5)	(6)	(7)	(8)	(9)	(10)	(11)
(1) Vietnam service	−.220	.188	.256	−.128	.183	−.108	−.096	.134	−.150	−.063
(2) Effective personnel manipulation		−.190	−.174	.419	−.216	.222	−.131	.098	.163	.148
(3) Time in service			−.079	−.218	.126	−.069	.103	−.003	−.174	−.110
(4) Branch of service				−.069	.033	−.006	−.078	−.092	−.123	−.094
(5) Avoided conscription					−.188	.279	−.109	−.009	.175	.075
(6) Favored war						−.125	.140	.012	−.121	−.065
(7) Parents opposed draft							−.167	−.045	.061	.066
(8) Age								.095	.171	−.080
(9) Race									.270	.306
(10) Education										.234
(11) Social class										

Table 7-9.   **Partial Regression Coefficients and Betas for the Determinants of Vietnam Service (NDS)**

	Partial Regression Coefficient	Partial Beta
Effective personnel manipulation	− .060	− .124
Time in service	.070	.176
Branch of service	.233	.225
Favored war	.177	.145
Age	− .017	− .124
White	− .098	− .090

Table 7-10.   **Multiple Regression Results for Five Variables in Vietnam Service Model (NDS)**

Dependent Variable	Percentage of Variance Explained	Independent Variable	Partial Regression Coefficient	Partial Beta
Effective personnel manipulation	22	Avoid	.747	.360
		Favored war	− .333	− .131
		Parents opposed draft	.296	.104
		White	.187	.083
		Social class	.100	.081
Time in service	8	Effective personnel manipulation	− .112	− .092
		Avoid	− .359	− .142
		Education	− .130	− .151
		Age	.034	.101
Branch of service	4	Effective personnel manipulation	− .073	− .158
		Education	− .032	− .097
Avoid	13	Favored war	− .157	− .128
		Parents opposed draft	.329	.240
		Education	.054	.158
		Age	− .011	− .077
Favored war	5	Parents opposed draft	− .102	− .092
		Education	− .039	− .141
		Age	.016	.149

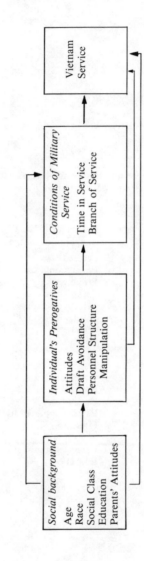

Figure 7-11.   Theoretical Model of Vietnam Service

Table 7-12.   **Correlation Coefficients between Attitudinal Variables (NDS)**

	(2)	(3)	(4)	(5)	(6)
(1) Military fair	.707***	.478***	−.185***	.240***	.280***
	(542)	(292)	(527)	(548)	(545)
(2) Military fair		.541***	−.270***	.237***	.218***
to friends		(289)	(523)	(545)	(542)
(3) Favorable effect on			−.365***	.440***	.245***
government attitude			(283)	(296)	(294)
(4) Try harder to avoid				−.147***	−.168***
Vietnam service				(533)	(531)
(5) National					.369***
purpose					(553)
(6) Personal benefit					

*Significant at .05 level.

**Significant at .01 level.

***Significant at .001 level.

Table 7-13.   Correlation Coefficients between Attitudinal Variables and Social Background Variables (NDS)

	Age	White	Parents Opposed Draft	Avoided Draft	Education	Social Class	Favored War
Military fair	.199***	.089*	-.083*	.032	.075*	.036	.148***
	(543)	(549)	(543)	(476)	(550)	(544)	(549)
Military fair to friends	.213***	.144***	-.160***	-.182***	-.013	.014	.131***
	(539)	(545)	(539)	(472)	(546)	(540)	(545)
Favorable effect on government attitude	.186***	.020	-.082	-.262***	-.178***	-.142**	.232***
	(294)	(296)	(292)	(250)	(296)	(292)	(295)
Try harder to avoid Vietnam service	-.117**	-.097**	.059	.162***	-.057	-.061	-.089*
	(527)	(533)	(528)	(464)	(534)	(528)	(533)
National purpose	.210***	.048	-.175***	-.214***	-.106**	-.089*	.331***
	(550)	(556)	(550)	(484)	(557)	(551)	(556)
Personal benefit	.080*	.028	-.170***	-.156***	.032	-.007	.182***
	(547)	(553)	(548)	(482)	(554)	(549)	(553)

*Significant at .05 level.

**Significant at .01 level.

***Significant at .001 level.

Table 7-14. **Correlation Coefficients between Attitudinal Variables and Military Career Variables (NDS)**

	Drafted	Time in Service	Vietnam Service	Combat Service	Personnel Manipulation
Military fair	−.093*	.139***	−.082*	−.097	−.060
	(349)	(545)	(531)	(225)	(499)
Military fair	−.074*	.163***	−.040	−.042	−.159***
to friends	(545)	(541)	(528)	(223)	(495)
Favorable effect on	−.024	.256***	−.066	.107	−.184***
government attitude	(295)	(294)	(286)	(135)	(272)
Try harder to avoid	.079*	−.018	.230***	−.025	.145***
Vietnam service	(533)	(529)	(518)	(224)	(494)
National purpose	−.071	.253***	.135***	.172**	−.198***
	(556)	(552)	(538)	(226)	(505)
Personal benefit	−.130***	.179***	.065	.126*	−.188***
	(553)	(549)	(536)	(225)	(503)

*Significant at .05 level.

**Significant at .01 level.

***Significant at .001 level.

Notes

Chapter One. Theoretical Perspectives.

1. The first two books in this series are Lawrence M. Baskir and William A. Strauss, *Reconciliation after Vietnam: A Program of Relief for Vietnam-Era Draft and Military Offenders* (Notre Dame: University of Notre Dame Press, 1977), and *Chance and Circumstance: The Draft, the War, and the Vietnam Generation,* (New York: Alfred A. Knopf, 1978).

2. Samuel Stouffer et al., *The American Soldier* (Princeton: Princeton University Press, 1949), I, 51.

3. A description of Durkheim's functionalism is found in Jonathan Turner, *The Structure of Sociological Theory,* (Homewood, Ill.: Dorsey Press, 1978), 25–28.

4. The distinction between societal and communal action is stated in *From Max Weber: Essays in Sociology,* trans. and ed. H. H. Gerth and C. Wright Mills (London: Oxford University Press, 1946), 180–252.

5. S. L. A. Marshall, *Men Against Fire* (Washington, D.C.: Infantry Journal, 1947).

6. Stouffer et al., *The American Soldier,* 106–12.

7. Stouffer et al., 112–22.

8. Edward Shils and Morris Janowitz, "Cohesion and Disintegration in the Wehrmacht in World War II," *Public Opinion Quarterly* 12 (1948): 280–315.

9. Roger M. Little, "Buddy Relations and Combat Performance," in *The New Military: Changing Patterns of Organization,* ed. Morris Janowitz (New York: Russell Sage Foundation, 1964), 195–223.

10. Charles Moskos, *The American Enlisted Man* (New York: Russell Sage Foundation, 1970).

11. John Helmer, *Bringing the War Home: The American Soldier in Vietnam and After* (New York: Free Press, 1974). Secrecy and supply as factors which must be overcome by a marijuana subculture are discussed in Howard S. Becker, *Outsiders: Studies in the Sociology of Deviance* (New York: Free Press, 1973). See also, Clifton Bryant, *Khaki-Collar Crime: Deviant Behavior in the Military Context* (New York: Free Press, 1979).

134

12. Edward Shils, "A Profile of the Military Deserter," *Armed Forces and Society* 3 (Spring, 1977): 427–32.

13. Stouffer et al, 139.

14. Ron Kovic, *Born on the Fourth of July* (New York: Pocket Books, 1977), 184. Another description of veteran demonstrations at the 1972 Republican Convention in Miami can be found in Hunter S. Thompson, *Fear and Loathing on the Campaign Trail '72* (New York: Popular Library, 1973), 382–92.

15. Lieutenant Colonel William Hauser, *America's Army in Crisis* (Baltimore: John Hopkins University Press, 1973). Another look with a similar portrait of the American military at the end of the Second Indochina War is David Cortright, *Soldiers in Revolt* (Garden City, N.Y.: Anchor Press/Doubleday 1975).

16. Shils and Janowitz, "Cohesion and Disintegration. . . ."

17. Paul L. Savage and Richard A. Gabriel, "Cohesion and Disintegration in the American Army: an Alternative Perspective." *Armed Forces and Society* 2 (Spring, 1976): 340–76.

18. Richard Boyle, *Flower of the Dragon* (San Francisco, Cal.: Rampart Press, Inc., 1972); Guenter Levy, "The U.S. Experience in Viet Nam," in Sam Sarkesian, ed., *Combat Effectiveness* (Beverly Hills, Cal.: Sage, 1980), 94–106.

19. Helmer, *Bringing the War Home.*

20. Moskos, *The American Enlisted Man.*

21. Gerth and Mills, "Introduction" to *From Max Weber,* 50.

22. Stanley Aronowitz, *False Promises: The Shaping of American Working Class Consciousness* (New York: McGraw-Hill, 1973).

23. Karl Marx and Frederick Engels, *The Economic and Philosophic Manuscripts of 1844,* ed. Dirk J. Struik and trans. Martin Milligan (New York: International Publishers, 1964). Another discussion of alienation can be found in Marx and Engels, *The German Ideology,* Part One (New York: International Publishers, 1970). An excellent secondary source on Marx's concept of alienation is Bertell Ollmann, *Alienation: Marx's Conception of Man in Capitalist Society* (Cambridge: Cambridge University Press, 1971).

24. Marx and Engels, *German Ideology.*

25. Marx and Engels, *The Economic and Philosophic Manuscripts of 1844.*

26. Gerth and Mills, "Introduction" to *From Max Weber.*

27. Quotes on this subject from Robert E. Lee can be found in Presidential Clemency Board, *Report to the President* (Washington, D.C.: U.S. Government Printing Office, 1975), 370.

28. Leon Trotsky, *My Life: An Attempt at an Autobiography* (New York: Pathfinder, 1970), 400–402.

29. Morris Janowitz, *Social Control in the Welfare State* (New York: Elsevier, 1976).

30. Durkheim's emphasis on the "moral" aspects of society can be found in Emile Durkheim, *The Division of Labor in Society,* trans. George Simpson (Glencoe, Ill.: Free Press, 1960). This author is indebted to Trent Schoyer, "A Reconceptualiza-

tion of Critical Theory," *Radical Sociology,* ed. J. David Colfax and Jack L. Roach (New York: Basic Books, 1971), 132–148. According to Schoyer, Habermas describes how the methods with which humans structure their thinking limit social action alternatives.

31. James Coleman, *Mathematics of Collective Action* (Chicago: Aldine, 1973).

32. James Coleman, *Power and the Structure of Society* (New York: W. W. Norton and Company, 1974).

33. M. Brewster Smith, "Competence and Socialization," in *Socialization and Society,* ed. John A. Clausen (Boston: Little, Brown & Company, 1968).

34. Melvin Kohn, *Class and Conformity* (Homewood, Ill.: Dorsey Press, 1969).

35. Albert J. Mayer and Thomas F. Hoult, "Social Stratification and Combat Survival," *Social Forces* 34 (December, 1955): 155–59.

36. Maurice Zeitlin, Kenneth Lutterman, and James Russell, "Death in Vietnam: Class, Poverty, and the Risks of War," *Politics and Society* 3 (Spring, 1973): 313–28.

37. Gilbert Badillo and G. David Curry, "The Social Incidence of Vietnam Casualties: Social Class or Race?" *Armed Forces and Society* 2 (Spring, 1976): 397–406.

Chapter Two. Foundations.

1. Baskir and Strauss, *Reconciliation After Vietnam,* and *Chance and Circumstance.*

2. During the Second Indochina War, there was a shortage of Non-Commissioned Officers (NCOs). To meet this shortage the military set up special leadership schools which would take a promising young soldier with only a few months in the Army and turn him into an NCO. They were often called "instant NCOs" or "shake and bakes." Many career military men were not very excited about the American military's task of "winning hearts and minds" in Indochina. Yet, for a war to occur and a career man to miss it was unheard of. Hence, a number of "old-timers," or "lifers" as they were usually called, volunteered for Vietnam service so that the appropriate entry would be on their records. At some future promotion hearing, the reviewers would then be able to note that these men had "had their tickets punched." That a man was a "lifer" was not necessarily any indication of disrespect. In Indochina, respect hinged on a leader's competence and his fairness.

3. Other researchers who have made similar conclusions to those of Baskir and Strauss include Helmer, *Bringing the War Home* and Savage and Gabriel, "Cohesion and Disintegration in the American Army: An Alternative Perspective."

4. Descriptions of Project 100,000 can be found in Baskir and Strauss, *Chance and Circumstance,* 122–31; Paul Starr, *The Discarded Army: Veterans After Vietnam* (New York: Charterhouse, 1973), 185–97; and Peter Barnes, *Pawns: The Plight of the Citizen Soldier* (New York: Warner Paperbacks, 1972), 66–68.

5. Baskir and Strauss, *Chance and Circumstance,* 123–27.

6. Category IV is the fourth category from the top in scoring levels for the Armed Forces Qualifying Test. The dividing line between Category IV and V, the bottom category, was usually the tenth centile. Sometimes Category V men ended up on active duty.

7. Baskir and Strauss, *Chance and Circumstance,* 152–66, and Starr, *Discarded Army,* 167–81, provide descriptions of the military discharge grading system.

8. The qualifications for a hearing by the Ford Clemency Board can be found in Baskir and Strauss, *Reconciliation After Vietnam,* 27–31.

9. Presidential Clemency Board, *Report to the President,* 80.

10. Seymour Sudman, *Applied Sampling* (New York: Academic Press, 1976).

11. Some of the material in this section was included in a paper presented at the Public Choice Society annual meetings in New Orleans in 1977.

12. Sol Tax, *The Draft: A Handbook of Facts and Alternatives* (Chicago: University of Chicago Press, 1967).

13. Presidential Clemency Board, *Report to the President,* 65. Readers with further interest in Post-Vietnam Syndrome should consult Robert Lifton, *Home from the War: Vietnam Veterans, Neither Victims nor Executioners* (New York: Simon and Schuster, 1973).

14. The 1970 percentages of armed forces personnel for each branch of service were calculated from *Statistical Abstract of the United States,* U.S. Department of Commerce, Bureau of the Census, 1971.

15. These quotes on Project 100,000 are from the Presidential Clemency Board, *Report to the President,* 54.

Chapter Three. Dynamics of Desertion: Crime and Punishment.

1. Uniform Code of Military Justice, "Article 85. Desertion" and "Article 86. Absent Without Leave" in *Manual for Courts-Martial,* United States (1969) pp. A2–26.

2. Baskir and Strauss, *Reconciliation After Vietnam* and *Chance and Circumstance.* D. Bruce Bell and Thomas J. Houston, "The Vietnam Era Deserter: Characteristics of Unconvicted Army Deserters Participating in the Presidential Clemency Board Program," Arlington, Virginia: U.S. Army Research Institute for the Behavioral and Social Sciences, 1976; and D. Bruce Bell and Beverly W. Bell, "Desertion and Antiwar Protest: Findings from the Ford Clemency Program," *Armed Forces and Society* 3 (Spring, 1977): 433–41.

3. Stouffer et al, *The American Soldier,* 130–46.

4. Baskir and Strauss, *Chance and Circumstance.*

5. Bell and Houston, "Vietnam-Era Deserter."

6. Baskir and Strauss, *Chance and Circumstance,* 38–39, Helmer, *Bringing the War Home,* and Savage and Gabriel, "Cohesion and Disintegration in the American Army," 346–47.

7. Shils and Janowitz, "Cohesion and Disintegration in the Wehrmacht in World War II," 280–315.

8. General Lewis W. Walt, a member of the Presidential Clemency Board expressed this opinion in a 1977 *Penthouse Magazine* article.

9. Presidential Clemency Board, *Report to the President,* 62.

10. Presidential Clemency Board, 62.

11. Baskir and Strauss, *Chance and Circumstance,* 144–45.

12. The designation "real world" was frequently used among American troops in Vietnam to refer to United States.

13. Presidential Clemency Board, *Report to the President,* xvi.

14. Baskir and Strauss, *Chance and Circumstance,* 116.

15. Theodore Hesburgh, "Introduction" to Baskir and Strauss, *Chance and Circumstance,* xii.

16. Stouffer et al., 120–21.

17. Robert Sherrill, *Military Justice is to Justice as Military Music is to Music* (New York: Harper & Row, 1969).

18. Baskir and Strauss, *Chance and Circumstance,* 162–65.

19. Treatment of Deserters from Military Service Subcommittee of the Committee on Armed Services United States Senate, *Report,* United States Senate (Washington, D.C.: U.S. Government Printing Office), 31–32.

Chapter Four. Dynamics of Desertion: Vietnam Service and Absence Offenses.

1. Helmer, *Bringing the War Home,* 29–41.

2. Baskir and Strauss, *Chance and Circumstance,* 113.

3. Martin Luther King Jr., *Where Do We Go From Here: Chaos or Community* (New York: Harper & Row, 1967), 36, called the war, "ill-considered."

4. Stouffer et al., *The American Soldier,* 114.

5. See Richard W. Seaton, "Deterioration of Military Work Groups under Deprivation Stress," in Morris Janowitz, ed., *The New Military* (New York: W. W. Norton & Company, 1969), 225–47.

6. Shils, "A Profile of the Military Deserter."

Chapter Five. Dynamics of Desertion: Four Special Types of Offenders.

1. Baskir and Strauss, *Chance and Circumstance,* 214.

2. David A. Manwaring. *Render Unto Caesar: The Flag Salute Controversy* (Chicago: University of Chicago Press, 1962), 29.

3. Baskir and Strauss, *Chance and Circumstance,* 15–17.

4. Herbert Hewitt Stroup, *The Jehovah's Witnesses* (New York: Russell & Russell, 1967), 29.

5. Donald Light, Jr. and Suzanne Keller, *Sociology* (New York: Alfred A. Knopf, 1975), 440.

6. Presidential Clemency Board, *Report to the President,* 244.

7. Baskir and Strauss, *Chance and Circumstance,* 87.

8. The significance of this finding will be discussed at the end of this chapter.

9. Baskir and Strauss, 122–31, 144–48; Barnes, *Pawns,* 66–68. There is an interesting problem posed by this result since Barnes estimates that fifty percent of the Project 100,000 participants were sent to Vietnam. Post-Vietnam desertion was apparently very uncommon among Project 100,000 personnel.

10. Josefina J. Card, *Lives After Vietnam* (Lexington, Mass.: Lexington Books, 1983). Card found that Vietnam veterans are more likely to suffer from physical and mental problems than other veterans and non-veterans. This book is a thorough statistical treatment of the life histories of one cohort of the Vietnam generation.

11. Presidential Clemency Board, 63. Development of the concept of PVS can be found in Lifton, *Home from the War;* Charles R. Figley, ed., *Stress Disorders Among Vietnam Veterans: Theory, Research, and Treatment Implications* (New York: Brunner-Mayel, 1978); and Charles Figley and Samuel Leventman, *Strangers at Home: Vietnam Veterans Since the War* (New York: Praeger, 1980). The ailment's current designation and listing (in the American Psychiatric Association's *Diagnostic and Statistical Manual of Mental Disorders*, 1980) is postraumatic stress disorder (PTSD).

12. Presidential Clemency Board, 53–54.

13. Ibid., 54.

14. Baskir and Strauss, 126–27.

15. George Knox, G. David Curry, and Caroline Juniper, "Ex-Offender Job Success and Military Service." Unpublished manuscript. Available upon request from the Safer Foundation, 10 S. Wabash, Chicago, Ill.

16. Shils and Janowitz. "Cohesion and Disintegration. . . ."

17. Baskir and Strauss, *Chance and Circumstance,* 121.

18. Treatment of Deserters from Military Service Subcommittee of the Committee on Armed Services United States Senate, *Report,* 32.

Chapter Six. Processes of Legal Avoidance: The Selective Service System.

1. Presidential Clemency Board, *Report to the President,* xv.

2. Baskir and Strauss, *Chance and Circumstance,* 231.

3. This conjecture may be further supported by the lack of a stronger relationship between going to school to avoid conscription and level of education (6-4).

4. Kenneth Keniston, *Young Radicals: Notes on Committed Youth* (New York: Harcourt & Brace, 1969).

5. Baskir and Strauss, *Chance and Circumstance,* 112.

6. An example of this theoretical perspective is Fritz Heider, *The Psychology of Interpersonal Relations* (New York: Wiley, 1958).

7. Robert K. Merton, *Social Theory and Social Structure,* rev. ed. (Glencoe: The Free Press, 1957), ch. 11.

Chapter Seven. Processes of Legal Avoidance: The Military Personnel System.

1. Badillo and Curry, "Social Incidence of Vietnam Casualties."

2. M. Brewster Smith, "Competence and Socialization," in *Socialization and Society,* ed. John A. Clausen (Boston: Little, Brown & Company, 1968), 270–320.

3. By using statistical controls, it is possible to separate the influence of being black on going to Vietnam from the influence of being poor on going to Vietnam. What the cited result means is that a man who was white and poor was more likely to go to Vietnam than a man who was white and not poor, while a man who was black and not poor was also more likely to go to Vietnam than a man who was white and not poor. This condition, of course, boded most ill for the man who was unfortunate enough to be both black *and* poor.

4. Badillo and Curry, "Social Incidence of Vietnam Casualties"; Zeitlin, Lutterman, and Russell, "Death in Vietnam."

Chapter Eight. An Additional Policy Note

1. The term "illusions of the epoch" is from Marx and Engels, *The German Ideology.* It refers to the tendency among historians to emphasize the actions of leaders as opposed to those of common people in the shaping of human history.

2. Mark Clark, *From the Danube to the Yalu* (Westport, Conn.: Greenwood Press, 1973).

3. This question is posed in Morris Janowitz, "The U.S. Forces and the Zero Draft" (London: Adelphi), paper No. 94.

4. David Halberstam, *The Best and the Brightest* (New York: Random House, 1973).

5. Edward Shils in his lectures on warfare repeatedly emphasizes the connection between manhood and military service.

6. A sociological profile of America's military cadre at the beginning of the Second Indochina War can be found in Morris Janowitz, *The Professional Soldier: A Social and Political Portrait* (New York: The Free Press, 1971).

7. Little, "Buddy Relations and Combat Performance," 195–223.

Bibliography

Aronowitz, Stanley. *False Promises: The Shaping of American Working Class Consciousness*. New York: McGraw-Hill, 1973.

Badillo, Gilbert and G. David Curry. "The Social Incidence of Vietnam Casualties: Social Class or Race?" *Armed Forces and Society* 2 (Spring, 1976): 397–406.

Barnes, Peter. *Pawns: The Plight of the Citizen Soldier*. New York: Warner Paperbacks, 1972.

Baskir, Lawrence M. and William A. Strauss. *Chance and Circumstance: The Draft, the War, and the Vietnam Generation*. New York: Alfred A. Knopf, 1978.

_____. *Reconciliation after Vietnam: A Program of Relief for Vietnam-Era Draft and Military Offenders*. Notre Dame: University of Notre Dame Press, 1977.

Becker, Howard S. *Outsiders: Studies in the Sociology of Deviance*. New York: Free Press, 1973.

Bell, D. Bruce and Thomas J. Houston. "The Vietnam Era Deserter: Characteristics of Unconvicted Army Deserters Participating in the Presidential Clemency Board Program." Arlington, Va.: U.S. Army Research Institute for the Behavioral and Social Sciences, 1976.

Bell, D. Bruce and Beverly W. Bell. "Desertion and Antiwar Protest: Findings from the Ford Clemency Program." *Armed Forces and Society* 3 (Spring, 1977): 433–441.

Boyle, Richard. *Flower of the Dragon*. San Francisco: Rampart Press, 1972.

Bryant, Clifton. *Khaki-Collar Crime: Deviant Behavior in the Military Context*. New York: Free Press, 1979.

Card, Josefina. *Lives after Vietnam: The Personal Impact of Military Service*. Lexington, Mass.: Lexington Books, 1983.

Clark, Mark. *From the Danube to the Yalu*. Westport, Conn.: Greenwood Press, 1973.

Coleman, James. *Mathematics of Collective Action*. Chicago: Aldine, 1973.

141

_____. *Power and the Structure of Society.* New York: W. W. Norton & Co., 1974.

Cortright, David. *Soldiers in Revolt.* Garden City, N.Y.: Anchor Press/Doubleday, 1975.

Durkheim, Emile. *The Division of Labor in Society.* Trans. George Simpson. Glencoe, Ill.: Free Press, 1960.

Figley, Charles R. *Stress Disorders among Vietnam Veterans: Theory, Research, and Treatment Implications.* New York: Bruner-Mayel, 1978.

Figley, Charles R. and Seymour Leventman. *Strangers at Home: Vietnam Veterans since the War.* New York: Praeger, 1980.

Halberstam, David. *The Best and the Brightest.* New York: Random House, 1973.

Hauser, Lieutenant Colonel William. *America's Army in Crisis.* Baltimore: Johns Hopkins University Press, 1973.

Heider, Fritz. *The Psychology of Interpersonal Relations.* New York: Wiley, 1958.

Helmer, John. *Bringing the War Home: The American Soldier in Vietnam and After.* New York: Free Press, 1974.

Janowitz, Morris. *The Professional Soldier: A Social and Political Portrait.* New York: Free Press, 1971.

_____. *Social Control in the Welfare State.* New York: Elsevier, 1976.

_____. "The U.S. Forces and the Zero Draft." London: Adelphi, Paper No. 94.

Keniston, Kenneth. *Young Radicals: Notes on Committed Youth.* New York: Harcourt & Brace, 1969.

King, Martin Luther, Jr. *Where Do We Go From Here: Chaos or Community.* New York: Harper & Row, 1967.

Kohn, Melvin. *Class and Conformity.* Homewood, Ill.: Dorsey Press, 1969.

Kovic, Ron. *Born on the Fourth of July.* New York: Pocket Books, 1977.

Lifton, Robert Jay. *Home from the War: Vietnam Veterans, Neither Victims nor Executioners.* New York: Simon and Schuster, 1973.

Little, Roger W. "Buddy Relations and Combat Performance." Pp. 195–223 in *The New Military: Changing Patterns of Organization.* Ed. Morris Janowitz. New York: Russell Sage Foundation, 1964.

Manwaring, David A. *Render Unto Caesar: The Flag Salute Controversy.* Chicago: University of Chicago Press, 1962.

Marshall, S. L. A. *Men Against Fire.* Washington, D.C.: Infantry Journal, 1947.

Marx, Karl and Frederick Engels. *The Economic and Philosophic Manuscripts of 1844.* Ed. Dirk J. Struik and trans. Martin Milligan. New York: International Publishers, 1964.

_____. *The German Ideology,* Part One. New York: International Publishers, 1970.

Mayer, Albert J. and Thomas F. Hoult. "Social Stratification and Combat Survival." *Social Forces* 34 (December, 1955): 155–159.

Merton, Robert K. *Social Theory and Social Structure.* Revised Edition. Glencoe, Ill.: Free Press, 1957.

Moskos, Charles. *The American Enlisted Man.* New York: Russell Sage Foundation, 1970.

O'Brien, Robert M. "Using Rank-Order Measures to Represent Continuous Variables." *Social Forces* 61 (September, 1982): 144–155.

Ollman, Bertell. *Alienation: Marx's Conception of Man in Capitalist Society.* Cambridge: Cambridge University Press, 1971.

Presidential Clemency Board. *Report to the President.* Washington, D.C.: U.S. Government Printing Office, 1975.

Sarkesian, Sam C. (ed.). *Combat Effectiveness: Cohesion, Stress, and the Volunteer Military.* Beverly Hills, Cal.: Sage, 1980.

Savage, Paul L. and Richard A. Gabriel. "Cohesion and Disintegration in the American Army: An Alternative Perspective." *Armed Forces and Society* 2 (Spring, 1976): 340–376.

Schoyer, Trent. "A Reconceptualization of Critical Theory." Pp. 132–148 in *Radical Sociology.* Ed. J. David Colfax and Jack L. Roach. New York: Basic Books, 1971.

Seaton, Richard W. "Deterioration of Military Work Groups Under Deprivation Stress." Pp. 225–247 in Morris Janowitz, ed., *The New Military.* New York: W. W. Norton & Company, 1969.

Sherrill, Robert. *Military Justice is to Justice as Military Music is to Music.* New York: Harper & Row, 1969.

Shils, Edward. "A Profile of the Military Deserter." *Armed Forces and Society* 3 (Spring, 1977): 427–432.

Shils, Edward and Morris Janowitz. "Cohesion and Disintegration in the Wehrmacht in World War II." *Public Opinion Quarterly* 12 (1948): 280–315.

Smith, M. Brewster. "Competence and Socialization." Pp. 270–320 in John A. Clausen, ed., *Socialization and Society.* Boston: Little, Brown & Company, 1968.

Starr, Paul. *The Discarded Army: Veterans After Vietnam.* New York: Charterhouse, 1973.

Statistical Abstract of the United States. U. S. Department of Commerce, Bureau of the Census, 1971.

Stouffer, Samuel, et al. *The American Soldier.* Volume I. Princeton: Princeton University Press, 1949.

Stroup, Herbert Hewitt. *The Jehovah's Witnesses.* New York: Russell & Russell, 1967.

Sudman, Seymour. *Applied Sampling.* New York: Academic Press, 1976.

Tax, Sol. *The Draft: A Handbook of Facts and Alternatives.* Chicago: University of Chicago Press, 1967.

Thompson, Hunter S. *Fear and Loathing on the Campaign Trail '72.* New York: Popular Library, 1973.

Trotsky, Leon. *My Life: An Attempt at Autobiography.* New York: Pathfinder, 1970.

Turner, Jonathan. *The Structure of Sociological Theory.* Rev. Ed. Homewood, Ill.: Dorsey Press, 1978.

Uniform Code of Military Justice. "Article 85. Desertion" and "Article 86. Absent Without Leave," in *Manual for Courts-Martial.* United States, 1969.

Weber, Max. *From Max Weber: Essays in Sociology.* Ed. and trans. H. H. Gerth and C. Wright Mills. London: Oxford University Press, 1946.

Zeitlin, Maurice, Kenneth Lutterman, and James Russell. "Death in Vietnam: Class, Poverty, and the Risks of War." *Politics and Society* 3 (Spring, 1973): 313–328.

Index